Start Small

A Quick Start Guide to Seeking the Kingdom

Karen S. Dilbeck

Forewords by Jack R. Taylor & Gene Edwards

Scripture quotations marked NIV are taken from THE HOLY BIBLE, NEW INTERNATIONAL VERSION®, NIV® Copyright © 1973, 1978, 1984, 2011 by Biblica, Inc.® Used by permission. All rights reserved worldwide.

Scripture quotations marked MSG are taken from The Message. Copyright © 1993, 1994, 1995, 1996, 2000, 2001, 2002. Used by permission of NavPress Publishing Group.

Scripture quotations marked KJV are from The King James Version of the Holy Bible. Public Domain.

Scripture quotations marked NLT are taken from the Holy Bible, New Living Translation, copyright © 1996, 2004, 2015 by Tyndale House Foundation. Used by permission of Tyndale House Publishers, Inc., Carol Stream, Illinois 60188. All rights reserved.

Scripture quotations marked JBP are taken from The New Testament in Modern English by J.B Phillips copyright © 1960, 1972 J. B. Phillips. Administered by The Archbishops' Council of the Church of England. Used by Permission.

Photos by Liz Bacon. Facebook: @Liz Bacon Photography Instagram: @liz_bacon with #lizbaconphoto

Cover photo by Serenity Mitchell from Unsplash.com

Bedford, Texas

Dedication

This book is dedicated to Tim,
the man I call my boyfriend,
but who happens to be my husband.
He still puts a skip in my step.

Acknowledgments

When I located my original composition notebook where I had scratched my first *Start Small* notes, I couldn't believe that over five years had passed. I didn't realize how time-consuming, nor tedious, nor satisfying writing a book could be. It truly was a fascinating process to gather my years of ponderings and revelations and place them within a book cover.

Thank you, happy family: Tim, Ty and Caroline, Jonathan and Emily, and Hamilton for being who you are. Each of you has brought a great measure of joy and the perfect amount of acuminating into my daily existence and for those two things alone I am in your debt. Thoughts of each of you bring the biggest, broadest smile to my face ... thoughts of you collectively make me want to cook!

Thanks to all the good people that let me use their stories, even though some of your names aren't spelled out, but still include: Aly Badinger, Piper Bedient, Rachael Boutwell, Robert Buffton, Kate Campbell, Tommy and Blanche Champion, Matthew Coyle, Hamilton Dilbeck, Jonathan Dilbeck, Tim Dilbeck, Ty Dilbeck, Carmen Falcione, Martha Givens, Natalia Gomez, Tammy Griffin, Dara Kolar, Daniel and Eunice Lee, Nat Lee, Bobby Magdon, Dalton Magdon, Gina Mangum, Annette Ntombuyenkosi Mucache, Pamela Neu, Janelle Rademaker, Kelsey Rhodes, Cary Shaffer, Danny Sillivant, Kay Sillivant, Gordon Sillivant, Stan Sillivant, Jack Taylor, Tim Taylor, Sharlene Thornberry, Sam Watson, Dexter Watts, Patricia Watts, and Kelly Sillivant White.

If there is such a thing as a special thank you, then it goes to my editor and worldwide traveling handler, Kate Campbell. You listened to my original vision with patient ears while allowing me to confess my weakness of scattered thinking. After reading and re-reading my manuscript, you spoke the hard things at the right time and encouraged me when I needed it most. I'm glad that our editing sessions included lots of chatting and good food. I'm also grateful that we never mentioned the fact that we edited each other's edits! Kate, you not only inspire me with your efficiency but, even more so, with your untethered quest to seek His Kingdom first—even in a parking lot. You're the best.

Thank you, Tim Taylor, for over ten years ago planting a seed in me by casually mentioning your company's tagline, "Everyone has a book in them." I knew I did, but you made me believe that it could be. Thanks for successfully navigating a 30-year-plus friendship through the publishing gauntlet ... and Michelle, thank you, just because it cost nothing extra to include you. You do what you do like no other!

Thank you to Pike Road Baptist Church (Pike Road, Alabama) for being the stealthy small church that God called us to be. To all of you, as well as to Jay and Mary Ruth Wolf and the people at First Baptist Church (Montgomery, Alabama), thank you for trusting me enough to let me teach Kingdom while personally hashing my way through it. Those years are priceless. Thank you, Tignall Baptist Church (Tignall, Georgia) for teaching me what unconditional and graceful love is. Thank you Ashley River Baptist Church (Charleston, SC) for nurturing a little girl straight into the Kingdom. My first 17 years with you set me on a path to know my Creator. For that, I am, quite literally, forever grateful.

Thank you, Seth Barnes, Bob Mudd, Bill Swan and all of the crazy Millennials and Gen-Z-er's at Adventures in Missions—you have fearlessly invited me to share my Kingdom findings and given me the privilege of planting many Kingdom seeds in small places all over the world.

Thank you, Liz Bacon, of Liz Bacon Photography, for the tiny photo of me on the back cover. I just wish I had more places to show off your talent!

Thank you to Serenity Mitchell for sharing your photos with Unsplash.com. When I first laid eyes on the bottled water, I simply knew that it was the one! Your talent is subtly audacious.

Last, but never least, thank you, God, for making me and making Yourself known to me. Thank you, Jesus, for inviting me in just like I am, and thank you, Holy Spirit, for hanging out inside of me. Life in this Kingdom is so much better than ...

Contents

Foreword by Jack R. Taylor

From the opening of this volume, I experienced emotions that seemed strangely between offense and irritation. At first, I couldn't figure it out. Offended at the thought of "starting small," something I considered impossible, in light of the size of this eternal and enduring Kingdom, I began to experience deliberate wishes to downplay the seeming down-sizing of the Kingdom. It seemed so, well so "little" and "nothing" and "small stuff." The growing irritation soon became a sizable offense. I was noticeably snagged by, "Where had all this come from? Where is it taking us from? Where is it taking us to?" My offense was ample enough to determine my reading it all—every word! Finally, after one stabbing offense after another, I finished the manuscript—again, every word of it—every painful word of it!

There I stood, a silent, stoic, steaming sentry, guarding a glorious subject against seeming abuse. Three questions lingered past the finish: Where from? Where at? Where to? Oh, I'm over it now. The fact is, I'm run over by it! God gave me a resounding answer to this painful dilemma. Where did all this, I had just read, come from? What was it doing to me? Where was it taking me? The answer: Childhood—no sight and no entry except by certified "children!" This is what comprises the Kingdom! Children!

Here is the answer! I have just written *The Cosmic Initiative*, my consummate book on the greatest subject in the universe, the Kingdom of God. It may well prove to be my magnum opus. I know it's good, but the book you are holding in your hands, though small, has a feature whose absence weakens the power of the whole Kingdom message. Karen Dilbeck is to be commended for refusing to allow us to get over being children. In our becoming children of the Kingdom, we are forever identified as just that, "children!" Over that quickly-drafted toddler, hear Jesus say it again, "'Let, the little children come unto me and don't forbid them, for of such is the Kingdom of God." Hear it again and don't forget it. What is the Kingdom of God? Little children in the service of the King!

Thanks, Karen, for reminding us that we "little children" make up the Kingdom of God. Therein lies our glory and therein lies the genius of the Kingdom of God. I had not omitted it, but I had emphatically lessened it. No more! Thanks, little sister Karen for being one of the admitted "little children" and being vocal about it, and mostly for speaking it out and living it out! We hear you! Watch us now!

Jack Taylor, President
Dimensions Ministries, Inc.
Melbourne, Florida

Foreword by Gene Edwards

Read this book. Why? Because it is central to a Christian's life. *Start Small* tells us what is central to the Christian faith and also how to seek the Kingdom of God.

I wish I had had this book when I was a young Christian. It certainly would have set the sails of my ship in a far different direction than did the first book I read!

I applaud the author of this book for choosing such a momentous subject and doing it clearly, practically, and most of all, simply. I could not help but think of Elijah when his servant said, "I see a cloud the size of a man's hand." Elijah immediately told everyone to prepare for a flood. This book may be like that cloud, but for your life, it may turn out to be a torrential river.

I would also like to say that Karen, wittingly or unwittingly, has just pioneered the books of the future. Books of the future must be brief, clear, to the point, and must fit in the screen of our ubiquitous cell phones. Karen has given us what could have been a huge book that would have discouraged the modern reader from finding the jewels which lie therein. Instead, she has given us the genius of simple, brief chapters that clearly tell us exactly what is central and gives us the how-to of the Kingdom of God and the way that we can practically and uniquely explore making the Kingdom central in our lives.

In every way, Karen has served us brilliantly and well in this book mined in gold. Not only would I urge you to read this small masterpiece, but I would urge you to tell others of your unique generation to also sip from its contents.

I am often asked to write a word concerning someone's new book. This is one of those times when I eagerly endorse a book. In *Start Small*, we can find a handful of the major issues of our Christian life.

Gene Edwards
Best selling Author

Introduction: The Wrong Questions

I discovered the *Kingdom* back in 1995. *Discovered* might not be the right word. Maybe *realized the Kingdom existed* would be more accurate.

I was a 37-year-old wife and mom. My 61-year-old mother had just died from a horrific cancer that had taken much of her jaw. I was not disillusioned in my faith, but admittedly, I was shaken.

When someone else's mom died from cancer, I was able to stand firm. This time cancer bit *my* mom; then it took her very life. I had questions. Some were about healing, or rather the lack thereof. Others were concerning my perception of her undeserved suffering. The realization of her simply *not being* was overwhelming.

In my grief, and because my prayers were seemingly useless, I went to the Bible looking for hope. I used my mom's Bible—an old hardback copy of the *J.B. Phillips New Testament* translation. It had her fingerprints.

I started reading at the beginning, in Matthew, looking for answers to my many why-questions. As God often does, He changed the conversation.

Frequently, God tends to highlight things for me, like people, items, and words. He draws my eye, as well as my mind, to stuff that I would normally overlook. It happens subtly, like a breeze. When this occurs, my spirit takes pause.

The same thing happened to the Psalmist David while writing his Psalms. When it did, he would pen the word *Selah* next to that verse. *Selah* means rest, take pause, pay attention. I was soon to learn that this happens all the time when walking with God.

Such was the case during my grief. I wanted my specific questions answered. He wanted me to see eternity.

Kingdom. That was the word that was highlighted—over and over and over—and not just in Matthew. As I read on, He showed me the thread:

John the Baptizer shouted that *the Kingdom* was near.

When Jesus started talking publicly, He said *the Kingdom* was here.

He added that prostitutes would enter *the Kingdom* before "righteous Pharisees."

And that one had to become like a small child in order to receive this *Kingdom.*

The Kingdom was also, by the way, a gift and, strangely enough, was inside of those who believe.

Oh, and this *Kingdom* wasn't something one could physically see or touch, but it was composed of "righteousness, peace, and the joy of the Holy Ghost."

To walk in *the Kingdom*, one had to be convinced that the last really would be first, and that the first really would be last.

Being a servant, turning the other cheek, and going the extra mile were *literal*, as well as figurative, responses that caused action in the heavenlies.

Ah, the heavenlies. Jesus clearly stated that *His Kingdom* is not of this realm, not of this world.

After Jesus rose from the dead, *the Kingdom* was the only subject He spoke about for that short 40-day period before He stepped off the earth and into eternity.

Then Phillip picked up where Jesus left off, preaching about the good news of *the Kingdom* and of the name of Jesus Christ.

Paul continued with great passion, describing how to get into and walk in *the Kingdom*. He also offered the warning that everything not of God's *Kingdom* would be shaken.

Over the next several weeks and months and years, my quest for answers turned into a personal crusade to clearly define and understand, or at least attempt to understand, *the Kingdom*.

Then, of course, to learn to actually seek it.

This book is not a theological essay. Rather, *Start Small* is intended to be plain and simple.

My desire in writing is to plant *Kingdom* seed that falls on good soil, with the hope that the harvest will be beyond your wildest dreams.

Karen

Part One

Defining the Kingdom

Chapter One

Going Through the Motions

"*P*lease stand and join me in reciting the Lord's Prayer," I ask, purposefully stoic.

It is at that very moment that the anticipated glazed looks appear on each and every face. The age, the gender, nor the ethnicity matters. The number of people in the room is of no consequence either, whether it be six or 600.

When the recitation begins, we are all simply going through the motions. The dullness is there. It arrives the moment that the phrase, *"Our Father, who art in heaven ..."* slips off our tongues and remains until the last line is uttered: *"thine is the Kingdom, the power and the glory, forever and ever. Amen."*

This is when the stupor is broken. I ask the group a simple question, "How many times did you say *Kingdom*?"

I can see that the rote prayer is running through their heads one more time. Eyes are squinting in concentration, and counting fingers are moving as, finally, someone blurts out, "Two! Is it three ...? No, it's two! Two times!"

Yes, two times.

Then comes the first of the two follow-up questions: "How do *you define* the Kingdom?"

After a period of fairly awkward silence the first, and usually only, response comes: "God's reign."

"Yes," I reply, "That is true. But I want more."

I nod as a few more good, and accurate answers hesitantly trickle in: "The place God rules," and "Heaven on earth ...."

Then I ask my next question: "Jesus tells us in Matthew 6:33 to *'Seek the Kingdom first.'* If we are having a hard time defining Kingdom, then how can we seek it?"

Magic Matter

If you can't explain it simply,
then you don't understand it well enough.
—Albert Einstein

Conjuring up an image of a kingdom is fairly easy. Even the most sheltered of us have been exposed to the idea of kingdom through television, books, video games and Netflix. It's not difficult to rouse visions of castles and kings, knights and round tables, serfs and servants, nasty guillotines, adorned horses, giant goblets of wine, overflowing banqueting tables, and, of course, the beautiful damsel in distress. These components pretty much describe a kingdom.

The *concept* of a kingdom is easy to grasp. However, the Kingdom that Jesus refers to over and over may appear ambiguous and distant, seemingly making it of no significance today.

When my sons were young, I found a recipe for Magic Matter, a substance made out of corn starch, water, and dye. If the substance is moved around in your hands, a ball can actually be formed. However, the ball quickly morphs into liquid and oozes right through your fingers. After all, the matter was called *magic* for a reason: it could not be contained.

Initially, when I became aware of the Kingdom and purposed to seek it, I thought that I had it right in the palm of my hand. At first, I thought I understood it. But that understanding would eventually morph and trickle through my fingers.

I was making the Kingdom too complicated, and unfortunately, too religious. I was trying to press it into a ball. The Kingdom doesn't tolerate that.

The quote by Albert Einstein taunted me for quite some time, especially since I noted that others were also struggling with simply defining the Kingdom. Therefore, I will explain my plain, still-evolving definition, as well as my personal understanding of, the Kingdom.

The Kingdom is:

God Himself as the King, the way things are done therein, and my role in it.

1. *God as the King.*

God is the one and only true God, the Creator of everything seen and unseen.

He has revealed Himself as three-in-one, what believers call the Trinity. The Trinity is often referred to in prayers, weddings, baptisms, and funerals: *"in the name of the Father, the Son, and the Holy Spirit."*

He is *the King* of this all-encompassing Kingdom. Everything that He wants to happen happens. Always. The motive for everything He does, causes, and allows is *love*. E V E R Y T H I N G.

Pursuing God is *seeking* the Kingdom.

2. *The way things are done.*

God does things a certain way. The Kingdom operates and functions *His way*, which is upside down to the way the world does things, or rather, the world is upside down to the way God does things.

His ways are not our ways.

Pursuing the ways of the Kingdom is key in seeking it.

3. *My role in the Kingdom.*

When I become a part of this Kingdom, I have a role in it. The role may be a certain function, an actual task, or to simply be an observer. The King either gives me something to do or nudges me to see something that obviously needs to be done. Sometimes my role is simply to *watch* what He is doing.

Because of the way He does things (*being upside-down to the way the world does things*), my role will often go unnoticed by others in the seen realm. Performing this role may seem infinitesimally small, almost as if not doing it won't even matter.

But it always matters.

The results may not be immediately realized and, often, the results may not even be noted. But, again, the role, or the task, matters. Trusting the King means I just simply *do it*.

Recognizing my role, wherever my feet are, is seeking the Kingdom.

The King, the way He does things, and my role are always intertwined and continually in motion. This means that actually *seeking the Kingdom* is always intriguing, mysterious, life-giving, and never-ending.

Chapter Two

God as King

This King of ours can produce a 72-degree Fahrenheit sunny day, beckoning people out of their houses. He can make the wind blow to prevent someone from burning a brush pile one day and can make it rain to delay a harvest the next. He can send lightning to stall a football game or can dispatch a snowstorm to keep troops in place. He does all of this with purpose and reason.

However, what we see is not actually as it seems, because what is seen is temporary and what is unseen is eternal. There is always more—more that we do not understand or comprehend. He made it so. The King's request of us is fairly simple, though not often easy. He says, "Trust me."

He is the Creator of the universe, and every minor detail is useful and intentional. No bird falls from the sky without Him knowing and caring, and He knows how many hairs are on each of our heads. He has and is unlimited storage.

This God, who is a God of order, also brings His order to the seen and unseen chaos that mankind chose to bring to this planet. It is His way of doing things in His Kingdom.

Too often we balk at the concept of an all-knowing, intricately involved God. Why? Because, though we try, it is too wonderful, and sometimes even too horrifying, for us to comprehend. It's easier for us to believe in the ability of the smartphone in our hand rather than in a sovereign, all-knowing, ever-present, unconditionally-loving God—a God who has chosen to reveal Himself to us as a loving Father, through His perfect Son, and by the way of the Holy Spirit who chooses to make His home in those who believe.

Father

I once got a sneak peek at a father's heart while at the beach in Thailand. I was one of the first ones on the beach that particular morning and was lying face down on my towel with an eBook in my hand. I was in my happy place. It was in that moment that I first heard the distant screaming.

It sounded far away. I thought maybe it was coming from one of the longboats that were tied up on the shoreline. As the howling continued, I sat up on my towel to more easily comb the beach and identify its source.

Ah, there he was: a young boy who looked to be about five years old. He was fully dressed in nice clothes and a matching little cap. He was located right on the shoreline. His clenched fists and stomping feet added a layer of intensity to his blood-curdling wail.

The *momma* in me felt a slight bit of panic as I impulsively sat up to study the rest of the beach, hoping to locate his mother. Whew, there she was, along with the little boy's daddy, both of whom were meandering about twenty yards in front of him.

By this time, I was blatantly staring. The parents were walking *away* from him, not towards him. I was now a silent observer in a classic battle of wills.

The child was immovable. His stomping and screaming continued to escalate. He truly had only just begun. Whatever he was fighting for was obviously worth the fight.

The parents, though, continued to move away, occasionally glancing over their shoulders, never losing sight of the boy on the open beach.

I noticed that one of the local workmen, like me, was a spectator. When our eyes met, he quickly pointed to the parents as if to say, *"The kid is OK, his parents are right over there. They have to win."* I nodded in agreement. He, too, was all in.

About this time, another man entered the scene. He was selling beautifully carved pineapple pieces on skewers and approached the little boy. He leaned down and held the enticing fruit in front of him as if to say, *"Take this. It will meet whatever your present need is."* The boy, momentarily, ceased from his screaming and eyeballed the skewer. The parents turned to watch the new player on this stage.

The child made a quick glance over to his parents. He now had their attention. He looked back at the fruit gift and made the unpredictable choice to swat at it. The splendiferous fruit had not appeased him.

The goal to conquer his parents was still squarely in front of him. Therefore, the wailing resumed. The pineapple man walked away.

I watched as the boy finally unplanted his feet and began to walk towards his parents begrudgingly.

However, they did not turn around. He screamed louder and stomped harder. All they did was walk and glance.

Finally, the boy began to run towards his parents. Slowly, the dad turned around. As the boy ran the father bent down, knees on the sand. Upon reaching his father, the boy pushed his own head into his dad's shoulder and leaned in. The crying turned into a whimper.

Though I was curious about the details of the battle, ultimately, it truly was about *wills*. No matter how loud the desperate wailing grew, the father had maintained his course. His perspective was so much broader than his son's.

The father reached for the son's hand, and the boy began walking next to his dad, following his father's steps, one at a time.

The show was over. The battle of wills had its clear winner.

As the King, God is the boss, the ruler of everything and, fortunately for us, He rules with a Father's heart. He so desires for us to walk with Him at His pace. He is a better father than any of our fathers. He is love, and He is loving. He loves us just the way we are.

One day while I was listening to my 70s playlist, I heard Billy Joel's song, "Just the Way You Are." I have listened to this particular song dozens, if not hundreds, of times.

However, on this particular day, I found the Father's heart towards me, towards us, the crown of His creation, in those lyrics:

I said I love you and that's forever
And this I promise from the heart

I could not love you any better
I love you just the way you are.

I knew in that very moment what it meant for Him to *sing over me*. This sovereign God created me and loves me *just the way I am*. Our King is the good, good Father.

In finding God in that song, as well as on that Thai beach, I also found the Kingdom.

Approachable

Jesus is God's son. He has been around since before the beginning. God sent him to the earth with many things to do, but with one specific purpose: *to die*.

When God enabled Jesus to rise from the dead, Jesus became my high priest. This is a cool way of saying that I don't need a preacher or a priest to get to God; I get to talk with Him directly.

The writer of Hebrews describes Jesus this way:

We don't have a priest who is out of touch with our reality. He's been through weakness and testing, experienced it all—all but the sin.
*So let's **walk right up to him and get what he is so ready to give. Take the mercy, accept the help.***
(bold, mine)
Hebrews 4:15-16 MSG

I once read this verse to a group of teenagers. I asked them if they had ever done anything that they didn't want to tell their parents.

Dalton, age thirteen, stuck his hand in the air and said, "ME!"

Of course, it was Dalton. "Tell me about it," I said.

"Well ..." he began without hesitation, "a couple weekends ago I got our fire extinguisher out from under the kitchen sink. I took it into the back yard and built a fire out of sticks and leaves ...."

My eyebrows rose as he continued, "... then I took the pin out of the fire extinguisher and put out the fire with it. Then I cleaned it all up so you couldn't even tell I was there. Then I put the pin back in the fire extinguisher and put the fire extinguisher back under the sink."

"Uh huh ..." I replied while I nodded my head. Dalton's story was not finished, and I was gut-hooked.

"Anyway, yesterday before my dad went to Walmart, he opened the cabinet under the sink, took out the fire extinguisher and said, 'It's empty.' He then left for Walmart, bought a new one, brought it home and put it under the sink."

What a dad!

This is where I jumped back in. "So, he never knew that you were the one that emptied it?"

Dalton smiled and proudly proclaimed, "Nope!"

"Are you going to tell him?"

This time *his* eyes widened at that suggestion. "Noooooo!" he said while shaking his head.

I continued, "Why not?"

Dalton quickly replied, "'Cause he'd whoop me."

With that phrase spoken, I went back to the verse I had just read from Hebrews and did a bit of relatable paraphrasing:

... because of Jesus taking our "whooping"
you can always go to God, and you can always know
that you will never get a "whooping."

We can always expect mercy and grace. Mercy, simply put, is *not getting* what you do deserve. Grace, on the other hand, is *getting* what you do not deserve.

Jesus the King is always approachable: all day, every day, any-and-everywhere, under any circumstances.

He simply wants us to come to Him in much the same way that He came to us: *willingly.*

Taking the Spooky Out of Spiritual

The Holy Spirit is the third part of the Trinity. I had heard Him referenced all my life. As I grew into my late teens, I heard curious stories of people falling out and speaking in tongues. Then in my later years, as I ventured into other churches and attended a wider range of meetings, I actually encountered these mysterious events.

People from the platform spoke freely of "hearing His voice" which didn't disturb me, but rather, just baffled me. So when I had finally became friends with one of these active listeners I took advantage of the opportunity to ask some questions.

Carmen was Italian and had the persona to match his heritage. His ready smile and the glimmer in his eyes complimented his bear hugs and bigger-than-life personality. He was known as the pastor's pastor in our town and he performed his unofficial role well.

Like most Italians, Carmen had a way of making anyone and everyone feel included and part of the family. He also never shied away from confrontation. One day, when I was a bit younger and cheekier, I confronted him about something that, frankly, had been bugging me since I had met him a few years earlier. He had just happened to become the target of my ongoing angst.

"Carmen, you're always saying things like, *'Well, God told me to do so and so ...'* and, *'I heard God say ....'"*

Carmen smiled and nodded, and I continued. "Exactly how do you hear Him? Because if I heard God say something, I'd remember every word He spoke."

Carmen was never short on words. However, before he spoke, he gave me a perplexed look as if to say, *"You should know the answer to this question."*

As best as he could, Carmen explained that God's Holy Spirit was speaking to him. Not in audible words, but in words that his spirit could comprehend and interpret. He was simply relaying what he had heard.

Up until this point in my life, my view of all things Holy Spirit was spooky at best. I hesitated to explore this part of God personally and chose to keep my distance from the spooky and stick close to things that I thought I could handle. So, since the Holy Spirit was also called the Comforter, I found a *comfortable* co-existence with Him.

I wasn't buying into the simplicity of what Carmen was saying. That is, I didn't buy into it until I realized that I, too, was actually *hearing* God's voice.

Since that conversation with Carmen I have realized that when someone enters the Kingdom (or as we commonly say, *becomes a Christian*, or *first believes in Jesus Christ*), they get this amazing gift of the Holy Spirit. With this gift, their once-dead spirit comes to life and is intertwined with His Holy Spirit who permanently lives in the one who now believes. This is what the Bible calls, the *mystery of the Gospel* or *Christ in me*. He doesn't just hang out in us; He moves in us and moves with us as we move with Him. He also leads and guides and teaches and comforts and abides (hangs out) in us. Yes, He speaks to us, Spirit to spirit. My role is not only to *hear*, but to recognize His voice over all the noise that daily confronts my head and my heart. Realizing the simplicity of this astronomical truth has taken the spooky out of the spiritual.

Learning to Hear

Martha and I were standing in the middle of a large meeting room filled with teenagers and parents all ready, but not willing, to leave such a jovial atmosphere. The room was consumed with talking, flirting, laughter, and movement.

In Martha's right hand, she held a bulky set of keys. I remembered an earlier conversation where Martha had told to me that she could simply jangle her keys and, if any of her three sons were in hearing distance, they would come to her. "I trained them when they were young. They know this sound."

"OK," I challenged. "Two of your boys are here. I wanna see it happen." Martha grinned and said, "Watch this."

Deliberately, with her thumb in the ring that held all the keys together, she swung them around her hand. The jangling noise occurred as they hit her palm.

I watch in pure amazement as both of her sons stopped what they were involved with and walked directly to her. Their ears had, indeed, been trained.

As they each appeared, they said, "What do you need?" She just smiled and winked at me. Mission accomplished. For me, the Kingdom found.

My ears can be trained to hear His voice. It is imperative to do so when walking in the Kingdom. Not only is it imperative; it is extremely life-giving and, well, downright fun!

The Holy Spirit in me is the same as Jesus Christ in me which is the same thing as the Kingdom of God within me:

> *The kingdom of God cometh not with observation:*
> *Neither shall they say, Lo here! Or, lo there! For,*
> *behold, the kingdom of God is within you.*
> Luke 17:21 KJV

This really is, as Paul said, the *mystery* of the gospel. We cannot figure out all of the details.

However, we each have the ability, no matter our age, or education, or station in life, to personally discover, or rather realize, more of how the Holy Spirit moves and works in each of us as individuals. He wants to lead and guide us, and if we purpose to train our spiritual ears to hear, then we can respond to Him whenever He speaks.

Since starting small is the primary way to do things in this upside-down Kingdom, then beginning a day with the simplest of questions: *God, what do You want to do today?* can alter a universe.

God is the King: God the Father, God the Son, and God the Holy Spirit: three in One—the Trinity.

Obviously, I, nor anyone else, cannot fully explain God. However, He is pretty adept at making Himself known. He chooses to communicate with us in a myriad of ways, all of which align with the way the He reveals Himself in the Bible.

Chapter Three

The Way of the Kingdom

Every family, every home, every neighborhood, every apartment building, every business, boat dock, tattoo parlor, sports arena, video game, and even table maker has a way of doing things. They have their own system—or lack thereof—their own preferences, their own likes and dislikes, and their own procedures and protocols that work for them.

For instance, in my house, if you don't like the way that I make biscuits, then you can leave ... or just not eat my biscuits. Over the years I have honed my way of making them. My family is thrilled with the way I make my biscuits. It works for us. So the highway is there for anyone who feels bothered with the way I craft them.

The Kingdom has its own way of doing things. However, the Kingdom is upside-down to the way the world functions (or rather the world functions upside-down to the Kingdom). It is totally opposite. It is contrary to our human nature. It doesn't make sense in the here and now, therefore making it illogical at best.

At first glance, the way the Kingdom operates is counterintuitive, but *seeking it first* changes our intuition dramatically.

Upside-Down

In the Kingdom, the first is last, and the last is first. In the Kingdom, the lowest position can absolutely be the most powerful position. In the Kingdom, taking the last place gives you a vantage point that is indescribable until you get there. In the Kingdom, choosing the small thing provides the most power. In the Kingdom, when you lose, you win, and when you get knocked down, you are actually moving forward.

The way of the Kingdom (how things function in God's Kingdom) is absolutely life-giving, just because it is so wildly simple.

Seeking the ways of the Kingdom (doing things God's way) not only changes each individual who opts to do so, but it also alters the spiritual, or rather the unseen environment.

Back to the Rote Prayer

Early on in my journey, I asked God to show me, in its simplest form, the way His Kingdom actually *comes*. In order for Him to do that, He had to show me *what* it comes into.

So He took me on a tour through some common Scripture that, unfortunately, had become too common.

It's near the end of Jesus's 40-day fast in the wilderness. Satan, as if on cue, arrives with three very specific temptations. The third temptation has to do with some rather appealing kingdoms that Satan points out from the top of a mountain.

The devil ... gestured expansively,
pointing out all the earth's kingdoms,
how glorious they all were ....
Matthew 4:8-9 MSG

God created me to be very curious as well as extremely visual. When I hear or read something, I see pictures in my head. So, in reading this Scripture with fresh eyes, this is what I pictured:

Jesus and Satan standing on a mountaintop in modern-day Nevada. Satan cocks his head slightly to the side and, lifting his finger, casually points towards the bustling, neon city of Las Vegas, noting how wildly incredible it is.

He waves his arm towards the casinos, the brothels, the theaters, the art galleries, the churches, the zoos, the LGBTQIA community, the football stadium, the top-notch medical facilities, the schools, the industrial parks, the city government, the skateboard park, the law enforcement agencies, the restaurants, the banks, and the shopping malls.

Each one of these entities has its own unique identity and reputation and cultural norms. In other words, their own *way* of doing things. They are all literal modern-day kingdoms within a kingdom. I then realized that the list could, and does, go on and on. So many kingdoms. So many sub-kingdoms. *These* are what the Kingdom comes into!

This mental image easily came into real life when I just opened my eyes. My three, now grown, sons were

41

attending college. Two of them were at the University of Alabama, and one was at Auburn University. I visited both of these institutions on several different occasions. It was during the course of one of these visits that I saw how Satan could be *gesturing expansively* to some pretty impressive stuff.

I noted that the kingdom of education was operative. Of course, we don't use the word "kingdom" in daily speech in the 21st century; rather we would more easily say "culture," as in, *"the culture of that school was that the boys were expected to wear ties to class."*

It didn't take a lot of effort to identify several of the educational subcultures on these campuses: science, business, communications, art, engineering, etc.

Each of those schools functions with their own unique culture. Another way to say it would be that each of those kingdoms has its own *way* of doing things.

When I walked a few blocks across the campus, I could see a football stadium, which, of course, possessed its own culture. On any given Saturday in the fall, you could find the functioning sub-cultures of the opposing football teams and cheerleaders and band members and officiants and trainers and custodial workers and scorekeepers and food vendors and, of course, the fans.

Each of these sub-cultures has its own method of operating, and each and every *person* in the stadium has a role on that Saturday within that culture. Each of these roles ultimately yields to the "king" (*the guy in charge: the head coach*) calling the shots from the sidelines.

One thing I gleaned while seeking *His Kingdom* on college campuses was the realization that each of us functions in many kingdoms (cultures and sub-cultures) and move freely between them every single day and often several times during each day.

The college students that were playing football or cheerleading had, more than likely, entered the kingdom of sports—the sports culture—when their parents signed them up for three-year-old mini-soccer years before. The sports kingdom, after all, offered many options as they grew up: soccer, basketball, baseball, volleyball, swimming, gymnastics, equestrianism, etc.

For some individuals, they were really good at some of the sports options. For others, not so much. Therefore, some kids dropped out of the sports culture (*sports kingdom*), only to find a new culture (*kingdom*), possibly art or science or hunting or video games or stealing or cutting grass or smoking pot, etc. Each of these options, of course, possess their own culture, with their own way of doing things.

Thinking about this for even a minute can lead deep into a rabbit hole. Simply put, *wherever my feet are at the moment is a kingdom.* For instance, if I were washing the dishes, then that particular space is a kingdom: I am the king, there is a way I choose to approach those dirty dishes, and I have a role, or rather a part to play in making the dishes clean.

Just as Satan suggested with his gesture, *glorious* kingdoms abound.

This new realization began to breath life into the rote prayer, *"Your Kingdom come ...."*

It also spurred more questions: how do I actually seek *the Kingdom*, His Kingdom, in the middle of all the kingdoms of this world?

Asking God for His Kingdom to come wherever my feet were, in whatever culture (or subculture) I was participating in at the time became normal. I was simply asking for Him to rule, and I was asking for His ways (or *the way* He does things) to be realized. I was also desiring to know my role during my time there.

Whenever someone is actually entrenched in, or simply a part of a culture or a kingdom, it is routine, even expected, to adapt to that culture's norms. This happens constantly and instinctively. It would be normal to yell and scream while at a football game. But, if someone yells and screams while waiting for a prescription to be filled at a pharmacy, security would likely escort them out the front door. After all, loud outbursts are not a part of the culture of the local pharmacy.

Adapting to the norms, or the way, of *His Kingdom* becomes routine as well.

Now, back to the mountaintop ...

Satan is continuing his expansive gesturing, pointing out all of the splendiferous kingdoms of the world to Jesus, while noting, "Hey, I am the king of all these kingdoms and if you kneel down and worship me, then, hey, they are yours ...."

Jesus doesn't kneel.

Instead He rather abruptly told Satan to leave, while adamantly declaring that only the Lord God was to be worshiped and served.

Jesus had a total understanding of what Satan did not.

Jesus knew the future. He knew that His very presence on the planet was ushering in God's Kingdom on earth. For, in only months, there would indeed be a transaction, but on a separate mountain top and on a totally different scale.

Chapter Four

My Role

I was desperate, and I wanted to do something to fix the situation I was in. I looked for just the right Bible verse and I was open to having worship music play in the background all day long if necessary. Maybe unearthing a thought-provoking quote would help, or maybe shaking a gourd—anything to make this *thing* better.

I was more than anxious and crazy-willing to do anything in order for my present situation to be altered. The hardest part was that it didn't feel like God was doing *anything*.

I had come to God more times than I could count. I laid out detailed blueprints of how He could fix this; I brought creative suggestions to Him that I just knew would make things right. I was well aware that He could just *speak the word* and my crooked world would be made straight again. But, alas, He would not.

Eventually, my prayers became more like groans—ambiguous at best.

Instead of giving Him options on how to correct this, I finally asked Him, "What do you want me to do?" *I needed to do something.*

The answer was swift. *"Nothing."*

The Holy Spirit does speak. All the time. Our role is simply to have ears to hear.

I know what I heard, Spirit to spirit. The word: *nothing.*

"Nothing!?" I nearly heaved. "I have to do *something!*"

His reply was immediate, "Doing *nothing* for you, is doing something. Do nothing."

So that was my role in this situation: to do *nothing*, which is what I did. I planted my feet and made the active choice to dismiss all my so-called solutions.

I did nothing. I didn't even hope anymore. I surrendered.

And then I saw Him work. He moved my mountain.

My specific *role* in this situation altered the way I approach the problems that arise in my life. I realized, first of all, that I am not smart enough to plan my reactions for each and every difficulty I find myself in, nor to figure out what Jesus would do. If I could, I would not need God Himself.

Secondly, I saw that I have a choice between suggesting ways for God to fix things, or asking Him what to do and then doing it. God does, indeed, have something to say about every difficulty.

I have a role wherever my feet are. That means that whether I am facing the death of a family member, or I am binge-watching *Survivor*, Season 82, I have a role, or a function there.

There are times that I ask God to tell me what to do, and there are times that He shows me what to do before I even ask. Very often the role He gives me is seemingly insignificant. But if my feet are there, *wherever they are right at the moment*, then He has me there for a reason.

I must be willing to ask Him: *What is my role in this place? In this space? During this time? What is my role while in this season, in this culture, in this sub-culture?*

I do have a role, a part, a job, something to do—even if He wants me to do *nothing*.

Here and Now

Seeking the Kingdom begins in the *place* that you are physically at the moment: sitting behind a desk, on a train seat, in a church pew, in a restaurant, walking down a street, hiking up the side of a mountain, laying in a bed, or on a beach or in the gutter, watching television, your computer screen, or the grass grow, chatting with a friend, or arguing with your significant other.

Seeking the Kingdom also begins in the cultures and subcultures (*the kingdoms*) that you are a part of. It could be your nine-to-five job, or the gym you visit weekly, or the health store where you regularly shop, or your school. If you are homebound and only interacting with a few people each day, or if you are active in an online gaming community, then you still have a role. If you play ultimate frisbee, or volunteer or teach school, or if you are a stay-at-home mom, a goat farmer, or unemployed, or a rocket scientist, then you have a role in that space, in that culture.

All of these *places*, all of these *cultures*, are kingdoms, and God has a role for each one of us in each of them. Most of the time our roles have something to do with God Himself, or with His people.

Part Two

Seeking the Kingdom

Chapter Five

Start Small

Jesus often did, said, and suggested some pretty crazy things, and I have often wondered if He enjoyed raising the eyebrows of his onlookers and freaking out His listeners!

One of His most unconventional teachings took place on the day He sent out His twelve disciples to heal the sick, raise the dead, and cast out demons. All in a day's work, right?

In this interaction, Jesus sounds like a tried-and-true army general shoring up his rather green soldiers. Yes, they were trained and ready, but Jesus was making this real.

The final instructions Jesus gives them for this particular mission put everything into perspective:

> *This is a large work I've called you into, but don't*
> *be overwhelmed by it. It's best to start small.*
> *Give a cool cup of water to someone who is thirsty,*
> *for instance. The smallest act of giving*
> *or receiving makes you a true apprentice.*
> *You won't lose out on a thing.*
> Matthew 10:42 MSG

Seeking the Kingdom can be puzzling. However, giving a cup of cool water is not. It's easy. It's an attainable task. Even a green recruit could do that.

So, I did that.

A True Apprentice

July in Alabama is hot. Real hot. Like choosing to stay inside where it is air-conditioned hot.

I was looking out the window while washing dishes inside of my climate-controlled house when I saw a middle-aged, uniformed gentleman crossing my neighbor's yard. I quickly concluded that he was not a thief, but likely a meter reader. God highlighted him to me, and the thought came, *"Take a cup of cool water to him."*

I didn't hesitate. This was doable. I shook the bubbles off of my hands. I ran to the fridge and grabbed a bottled water before heading out the door. He was, indeed, the meter man and he was crossing the street into my yard. I also noticed he was dripping sweat. Prime!

I slowed my eager pace down a bit so as not to scare him. "Sure is a hot day, isn't it?" I casually asked.

He responded with a slight smile and a nod.

I held out the water to him. "Would you like some water? I want to give it to you in Jesus' name." Dang. That sounded so religious. The words felt wrong even as they came rushing out of my mouth. I should have left off the last part.

He took the cool water with a "thank you." I smiled, turned, and hightailed it back into my house.

Handing someone a cup of cool water was dicier than I had anticipated. Yes, the task was easy, but I made it religious. I felt stupid.

However, I had done it. The door was open. I was a true apprentice who really had a lot to learn. I would not turn back.

The Kingdom is expansive and eternal. It is practical. It is not religious. It is not limited by space nor time. God invites us to partner with Him in it through the means of seeking it first.

It truly is best to simply start small.

Cary

It was years later that my husband and I began leading training camps for young missionaries. Part of our Kingdom teaching was to provide bottled waters to the millennials who were under our charge with a specific assignment: they were to ask God *who* to give it to.

We have done this with several groups, but one particular millennial stands out. Her name is Cary, and we were in Uganda. I did some teaching on the Kingdom and shared the verse about giving a cup of cool water and starting small.

While Cary was grabbing her water, she asked God, "Who?" His reply came quickly, "Children and women."

Women and children. Good. That was comfortable. It was shortly thereafter that she saw many women and many children. Each time she would start heading their way, she heard a clear "no" from the Holy Spirit. She passed a little girl wearing a worn Disney dress on the dirt road. "No." She passed a woman running a sewing machine in the heat of the day. "No." She walked past a brother and sister carrying heavy loads. "No."

It was then that she noticed a little boy with special needs sitting in the dirt. Cary just knew that he was her kind of special; yet, as she headed towards him, God, once again said, "No."

Cary was officially confused. Again, she stopped and prayed. She knew that He was now saying, "Outside of your comfort." And she asked Him to open her eyes.

She then approached a woman carrying a baby and offered her the bottle. This time, the woman refused the offering.

"What?"

She heard the word, "Comfort," in her spirit once more. And then she saw the one. In her own words she describes what happened next:

> *He was pushing his bike up the red dirt hill*
> *in his knit beanie cap. His load looked heavy, all*
> *bundled up behind his seat. While walking the road,*
> *we [had] passed [each other] three times.*
>
> *At the top of the hill, he stopped. He leaned his*
> *loaded bike on his body and took out a bottle of*
> *water with no more than three small sips. I stopped.*
> *"This one."*
> *I walked over, greeted him, asked about his day,*
> *heard about his journey, offered him the water, and*
> *wished him a blessed day.*
>
> *He was the one.*
> *"Yes, child. He was"*
> *I prayed. I listened. I looked. I prayed some*
> *more. I heard "no." I prayed. I looked. I listened. I*
> *was rejected. I prayed. I listened.*
>
> *I found the one He wanted me to find.*
> *I did not fully understand how deep or*
> *meaningful this moment was until we discussed*

[the assignment] as a [group] later that day.
You see, God led me to many individuals, but they
were not the individuals He had planned for me to
give my water bottle to.

God did, however, have a plan to teach me
through these individuals. He had a plan for these
individuals as well. I was not directed to give my
water to these women and children in my path. It
was hard for me at times, especially when I did not
give my water to the little boy with special needs,
sitting in the dirt.

But, come to find out, these women and
children where meant to be a part of another
story, another moment. My squadmates came
back with stories of how they had listened to the
Lord and gave their water bottles to the exact
individuals I was told not to give my bottle to.

Through this, God taught me to follow Him.
Follow Him. Listen to Him. Let the Spirit lead me. Be
okay with this. There will be times when He says "no"
but that does not mean the story is over.

The "nos" of my life may, in fact, be the "yeses"
of other peoples' stories ... other peoples' moments.

A true apprentice listens to the King ...

Chapter Six

Least, Lowest, and Last

From my bedroom, I could hear the exasperation in my dad's voice. "Hey! Where's the remote control?"

My dad rarely raised his voice. However, when he did, whatever each of us was doing became insignificant. Whatever *he* was doing became the priority.

The entire family hurried into the den, and few words were uttered as we all began to look for the missing remote control.

We each had our own way of seeking for it: Mom would shake the blankets and then fold them. My sister would shove all the newspapers to the floor. My big brother would lift and look under the sofa cushions. I would jam my hands into the back of the padded chairs.

Within minutes, my younger brother, obviously embarrassed, would walk into the room with the remote control in hand and apprehensively proclaimed, "I accidentally carried it into the bathroom."

Sigh.

After receiving the dreaded look from dad, my little brother placed the found remote squarely in dad's hand, and we, like little worker bees, all went back to our tasks.

After all, it was found.

Jesus clearly tells us to, *Seek ye first the kingdom* .... However, most of us are more skilled at looking for a television remote control than we are the Kingdom.

The Kingdom can be elusive, hard to pin down, and yet it is constantly here.

Similar to seeking a remote control, each of us will seek His Kingdom in a unique way. In other words, *my seeking* may not look like your seeking.

I have also discovered that there are many people who have been seeking the Kingdom without even realizing that they are doing so. I read their books and their blogs and their posts, and I listen to their sermons and podcasts and their Ted Talks. However, many of them seemingly have no realization that as they share their recent revelation, they have, in fact, found the Kingdom.

When you can recognize the Kingdom in the seeking—and the finding—everything shifts.

When my sons were young, they attended a basketball camp. On the last day of camp, it was announced that Jonathan, our middle son, had won an award for making the most foul shots that week. He held his certificate proudly as we snapped pictures.

Admittedly, though, we were a bit bewildered as to why he had not mentioned this notable accomplishment earlier in the week. "Son," we asked, "why didn't you tell us you were making so many foul shots?"

He shrugged his shoulders, and after some silence, innocently replied with a telling question, "What's a foul shot?"

Actually *knowing what the Kingdom* is exposes its significance. *Finding* the Kingdom is certainly pivotal to experiencing the life He intended for us to live.

This will sound cheesy, but when the Kingdom is found, today makes more sense and life is more satisfying.

When the Kingdom is found, this all-knowing God becomes less of an untouchable being and much more personal, purposeful, and enjoyable.

Actually realizing the vastness of what you have found is, simply put, beautiful.

Truly, the only way to begin to understand the Kingdom is to make the effort *actually to seek it*. The best way to begin is to *start small*.

The Least Person

... you don't talk to the water boy, and there's so much you could learn, but you don't want to know. You will not back up an inch ever, that's why you will not survive.

"The Underdog" by Spoon

I saw Janelle in the kitchen grabbing a quick snack. I began to tease her, "I saw you at the market ...."

She laughed.

The *market* that I was referring to was a mock-market held during the Adventures in Missions World Race training camp. It was an amazing re-creation of a conglomerate of outdoor markets from around the world. The purpose of it is to expose the participants to the noise, confusion, financial stress and language barriers of an authentic market.

During the faux-market, Janelle played the role of a crippled beggar with a baby. I had watched her as she sat on the ground and called out to the clueless, hurried participants shuffling past her. She had reached out towards them with one arm while with the other she held onto her wrapped-in-rags pretend-baby.

I continued with my observation, "... and I saw you stand up and walk closer to the action."

She laughed and explained, "Yeah, no one saw me sitting there, so I just moved right up in the middle of everyone."

"Did you ever get any money?" I asked, knowing that as a beggar, she wanted to get as much of the mock foreign currency from the missionaries-in-training as she could.

The levity dissipated as Janelle suddenly grew serious. "Nope. None at all. And, believe it or not, I only had brief eye contact with two people."

Sensing that the pretending was over, I asked, "Was that hard on you?"

Janelle's eyes began to tear as she answered, "It was one of the hardest things I've ever done. At first, I was begging for money—then food. No one even really saw me. Then I started yelling louder, *'WILL YOU PRAY FOR ME?'* Nothing. It felt horrible—and I was only a beggar for an hour and a half."

Her voice began to trail as she shook her head, "I can't even imagine ...."

In the Kingdom, the least person is tremendously valuable. And the least person isn't necessarily the ignored person, or the poorest person, or the ugliest person, or the person who mops the floor. Though, they could be.

The least person, on any particular day, could also be the most handsome guy, the most talented gal, or the richest old man. It could be the CFO or the secretary or the guy that empties your trash can every day. It could be your depressed Uncle Frank or your screwed up co-worker. Or it could be your mom.

Every day, each of us has access to a good number of people. These people either share space with us in an apartment or home, a classroom or causeway, an office or construction site, church or fishing boat, mall or sports arena, movie theater or coffee shop, sidewalk or hallway, concrete parking lot or highway.

The overlooked and unnoticed people are the ones on God's heart: *the least*. Each of the people that He highlights in front of us is a key to the Kingdom. Sometimes we choose to ignore His highlighting of them. Other times we don't.

Though neither my mother nor father realized it, both of them modeled seeking the Kingdom by looking for *the least*.

My mom used to stand at the back of her church each Sunday, surveying the room, looking for the *least person*. Normally this person was someone who was sitting alone or someone she had never met. She would walk up to the lone person and introduce herself. *"Hi, my name is Kay. Are you visiting today?"*

She would continue chatting with them and eventually ask if she could sit with them. My dad would join them later after teaching his eighth grade Sunday School class. After church, they would often take this new friend out to lunch.

It wasn't until my mother's funeral that I learned of her pursuit of these individuals. One by one they introduced themselves to me with similar stories:

I just love your mother. I was a first time visitor at
her church, and she came and sat with me
and then took me out to lunch.
We've been friends ever since ....

God highlighted a totally different type of person as the least for my father. He got in the habit of buying lunch on a regular basis for unsuspecting policemen. He would walk over to their table at the end of their meals, pick up their bill and go pay for it. I caught him doing it on several occasions.

Looking for the least person could mean holding the door open for someone struggling with groceries or writing a note to a sick co-worker. It may mean making coffee for your spouse when you haven't spoken to each other in two hours because of your latest fight. Or it could be sending your discouraged sister-in-law a gift via Amazon.

Looking for the least person means that you aren't considering yourself first; rather, you are consciously considering others *before* yourself.

The best way to look for the least person in your kingdom today is to ask God, *"Who is on your heart?"* He is quite capable of letting you know. Often He will let you know without you even asking. It is simply obvious in your *knower*. The King is pretty sharp.

All that is required from you is to have ears to hear and a willing heart to do what He tells you, or shows you, to do. Either will be obvious.

Looking for the least is merely one of a myriad of ways to actually seek the Kingdom.

Most mornings I ask God, *"Who is on Your heart today?"* Some days He will bring up the name of a person that

I may not have thought of for weeks, or months or, in some cases, years. Most days, He will answer with a question: *"Who are you meeting up with today?"* Other times, that person appears via a text, an email, or literally at my door, like a delivery person.

Whether I am meeting up with someone for coffee or counseling, or whether I am replying to a text or a knock on my door, it becomes obvious that *that* is the person who is on His heart.

I don't need to simply check that person off of my to-do list. That one person is important. That person is the one that He cares about, the one that He has called me to … to what?

That becomes the next question. *"God, what do You want me to do with this person?"*

As mentioned earlier, asking a question like this becomes a normal part of walking in the Kingdom, almost like grabbing your cellphone on the way out the door. It becomes the question to which He typically responds to something simple and always doable.

Sometimes it's *"really listen to them,"* or something more specific like, *"Ask them about their grief over the loss of their father."* Sometimes the answer is to take a gift to them or to pull them aside and say, *"Thank you for all you do."*

It is normally something *small*.

My role is just to do what the King tells me to do. If, and when, He tells me to do something, I know that I am a qualified messenger.

> *"When did we ever see you hungry and feed you,*
> *thirsty and give you a drink? And when did we*

ever see you sick or in prison and come to you?"
Then the King will say, 'I'm telling the solemn
truth: Whenever you did one of these things
to someone overlooked or ignored,
that was me—you did it to me.'"
Matthew 25:40 MSG

The Lowest Position

"I believe that God has *something great* for me to do," I uttered those words to a close group of friends when I was 30 years old, and I imagined myself being primed for the stage—possibly a sought after inspirational speaker?

Doing something great, to me, meant that I would be well-known and noticed. It is unclear now if I believed that that was what God wanted for me, or if I wanted it for myself. Did I want to do something great so that God and I could share the spotlight?

Since that time I have heard those exact words uttered by dozens and dozens of adults, young and old.

The subtlety of seeking greatness. The allure of recognition. The desire for bigger—desiring personal greatness—is upside-down to the Kingdom. In the Kingdom, the lowest position is actually the prime position, and it is the one we should be seeking. God will sometimes give us positions of greatness. However, *seeking the lowest position*, even in the middle of greatness, is actually seeking the Kingdom.

Something great in His Kingdom may be small in its beginnings with the potential of remaining small. If that is what the King desires and regards as necessary, then that is what matters. My main role is to trust Him.

Choosing the lowest position takes a conscious effort. It takes a brief moment to assess the room and take the least desirable seat or do the job that no one wants. It is in this choosing that our hearts are revealed. Am I too good for that? Do I care what others will think? Is that beneath me? Have I gotten to a place in my life where I believe that I have worked myself out of *those* roles?

In the Kingdom, those jobs are the jobs that God has set up for us to do. His eyes glance towards them, showing us where He wants us to sit and what He wants us to do. It is in doing that small thing, that undesirable thing, that the Kingdom makes sense.

I was asked to speak at an event for in Nicaragua. Most of the 75 participants slept in their tents which were set up on a large covered basketball court. Our hosts had just installed a new bathroom toilet, and our group was the first to use it. However, after the first day of being used, it was discovered that the incline in the laid pipe was not angled correctly, so things began to back up.

Since the fix would take a few hours, the guys were instructed to go in the woods. A bucket was placed in the enclosed bathroom for the girls. The plan was in place.

After a few hours, I jumped in line to take advantage of the make-shift facilities. However, when I entered the tiny room, the bucket was nearly overflowing. I tried to pick it up to empty it but realized that I didn't have the muscle for it.

So I quickly exited the bathroom and informed the others standing in line, "The bucket's full. I gotta find someone to empty it."

With a snarky grin, Matthew, one participant whom I knew well, quite sincerely said, "Hey, get Nat to do it. He doesn't mind doing stuff like that."

He easily interpreted my raised eyebrows as I lightheartedly replied, "Nat, eh ...?"

He, too, laughed at the unsaid implications. After all, he had been fairly indoctrinated into Kingdom living: least person, lowest position, last place.

I left him with one of my looks and headed off to find a local staff member to help.

As I headed back with help, I heard Matthew's voice *"Move out of the way!"* Then I watched as he, with both bands, maneuvered past me with the sloshing bucket, trying to move as quickly as possible without spilling a drop.

I know he heard me shout as he went behind the building to dump the bucket, "Matthew! You are the MAN! I am so proud of you! You get the Kingdom award today!"

Matthew had chosen wisely.

A few years later, while in Costa Rica, I met a young woman named Natalia. She had helped me with a wireless microphone a few times and she had donned a hairnet to serve meals in the food line. On my last morning there, she wanted to know what my husband and I actually *did*. I briefly explained that we worked with a leadership team. She was thrilled to learn that as, she too, was working with her local leadership team—training and speaking.

It was then that she asked if I had any advice for her since she was only 22-years-old and was at the beginning of her journey. The short answer appeared in my spirit immediately: "Natalia, always be willing to don a hairnet as easily as you would grab a microphone. *That* is the Kingdom."

Whoever wants to be great must become a servant.
Whoever wants to be first among you must be
your slave. That is what the Son of Man has done:
He came to serve, not be served—
and then to give away his life in exchange
for the many who are held, hostage.
Matthew 20:25-28 MSG

The Last Place

One time my good friend Dexter helped out with a children's event at our church. His job? To hand out candy at closing time. He held the bag up high and told the kids to get in line. After a little pushing and shoving the oldest, biggest, and strongest kids made their way to the front of the line. After the kids settled down, Dexter shouted, "The first will be last, and the last will be first!" He then sauntered back to the end of the line where all of the smallest and youngest kids received him gladly.

Ah, the Kingdom.

It doesn't feel normal to take the back seat at a concert. Or to sit on a couch with a plate of food when there are still a few seats at the table. It feels odd to let people through in traffic even when you're in a hurry.

But this is what it means to take the last place—to start small.

The opportunity to choose the last place can occur in a grocery store, a food line, a sporting event, or walking into a building. God gives us daily promptings to seek the Kingdom in these ways.

One afternoon I received a text from Kate, who had recently captured seeking the Kingdom:

I had a Kingdom moment today ... I pulled into the parking lot and saw that the front spot was open and was so excited and even thought, "Well the Lord has favor on me this morning!" ... But then I just heard Him say "Least, last, lowest ..." So I drove away and parked at the farthest spot.

Jesus puts it this way:

When you're invited to dinner, go and sit at the last place. Then when the host comes he may very well say, "Friend, come up to the front." That will give the dinner guests something to talk about! What I'm saying is, If you walk around with your nose in the air, you're going to end up flat on your face. But if you're content to be simply yourself, you will become more than yourself.
Luke 14:10-11 MSG

Seeking the Kingdom is relatively easy if you have ears to hear. Finding our role in the Kingdom is absolutely life-giving. This King, who is particular about doing things a certain way, has a role for anyone with ears to hear.

In doing so, we find the identity that we all long for, simply because true identity is found in knowing that you are known by your Maker and that He does, indeed, see *everything*.

Chapter Seven

Those People

He was teaching while on the side of a mountain. And He was on a roll, addressing nearly every topic imaginable. He was getting up in everybody's business. He was clearly and quite simply, explaining the way the Kingdom functions. And who better to explain God's heart than God's son?

Matthew, chapter five, is often referred to as the Sermon on the Mount. Jesus didn't call it the Sermon on the Mount, but that is what we call it.

The entire chapter paints the real possibility of a peaceful existence, a modern day Garden of Eden. Jesus is verbally setting the backbone of reality straight again. Yet, it was and still is, hard to fathom what He was suggesting. What He was presenting was unheard of then, and still is now. And yet the people knew in their knower that *life* was flowing through Jesus's very words.

Were the things He was proposing even attainable?

The bulk of what Jesus was suggesting, what He was teaching, seemed ludicrous, even foolish. No wonder people accused him of being insane. He talked quite literally, and yet also figuratively. Two-for-one while seeking the Kingdom. Here is a small portion of it:

> *You have heard that it was said, "Eye for eye, and tooth for tooth." But I tell you, do not resist an evil*

person. If anyone slaps you on the right cheek, turn to them the other cheek also. And if anyone wants to sue you and take your shirt, hand over your coat as well. If anyone forces you to go one mile, go with them two miles.

Matthew 5:39-41 NIV

We've shortened these verses to three quick phrases: *turn the other cheek, go the extra mile,* and *give them your coat.* All three have become catchphrases that are easy to say, but rarely done. Purposing to *actually do* them is *seeking the Kingdom.*

I took the time to truly consider how these three things looked in my own little kingdom. When I thought of turning an actual cheek an incident from son's high school years came to mind.

Oh, Seventeen

It was his first teenage fight. And there was absolutely was no way that I was going to persuade my then seventeen-year-old son to turn his other cheek after being hit in the face. That wasn't going to happen. Honestly, I didn't want him to be a punching bag. Could turning the other cheek be a practical option?

Each of us is accountable for our own self. So my son, who was knocking on the door of adulthood, was responsible for his actions as well as his reactions. From a mother's point of view, my advice was sound, but at his age, it would likely be disregarded.

What if I were hit in the face? Then I would have my own choices to make. After all I, too, am responsible for my actions as well as *my reactions*.

So I asked God to explain what turning the other cheek means for me. He clearly spoke to my spirit in a few short words: *"Turning the other cheek means you don't win."*

This line, *"you don't win"* explains the heart of the Kingdom, of which I am not the center. Jesus is.

I pondered this for weeks: *I don't win.*

I don't win, and I don't set out to win.

A sports enthusiast cannot get bogged down here—a game is meant to be won; not at all costs, but the *goal*, after all, is to have a winner.

However, for those with competitive spirits—those who purpose to win everything, every time, at all costs— you are accountable for you, in and outside of the contest.

In my time working with teenagers, I often hosted Dirty Santa parties, also known as White Elephant, Yankee swap, or a Cutthroat Christmas gift exchange. Basically, each person in attendance contributes a wrapped gift, and after a lot of gift-swapping per game rules, each person goes home with a different gift than they brought to the party. The catch? Some gifts are junk while other gifts are treasures. The ultimate goal is to take home a treasure.

When I asked some of the teenagers' parents to help with the game, I gave them strict instructions. "We, as adults, don't get to take home a good gift. In other words, *we don't win!"*

Bewildered stares appeared on two parents' faces who were known for their competitive natures. One parent verbalized her thoughts. "You're telling us to lose?"

I shrugged my shoulders and responded, "I'm telling you that I want us, as the adults in the room, to go home with the junky gifts."

The angst was evident. Her unspoken life mantra, to win everything, every time, at all costs, grated against the concept of her losing this gift swap. However, I had clearly stated the way this game was going to operate for the adults in the room: *we don't win.*

Not winning was ridiculously difficult for both of them. And, I confess, I judged them when they struggled. I gave them dirty looks when they forgot the instructions. I, not so delicately, tried to shame them for their forgetfulness.

I was proud that *purposing not to win* came easy for me. After all, I am not very competitive.

But then again, I do love to win an argument, to be victorious in a disagreement, and to be found right when I've been wronged. When there are just two of us, I will hold my jaw like a stone; there is no hint of *turning the other cheek.*

I found it simple to instruct my freshly-adult son in a biblical lesson for his bruised face, and I found it easy to tell others to lose a game purposefully. However, when confronted with an offense, I had my own feet planted, and my own fists clenched. I found it effortless to punch back—metaphorically, of course. *I had to win.*

But did I? Do I?

In this upside-down Kingdom, turning the other cheek means *I do not win.* However, in the end, when all has been said and done, I actually *am* the winner—for not winning. That's *the way* the Kingdom works.

Paper Mache Giraffes

A dear friend who is a high school teacher texted me and asked how the book was coming along. I told her of my struggle with the practicality of these three concepts: *turn the other cheek; if someone wants your shirt, give him your coat as well;* and *go the extra mile.*

I continued texting, "Hey, ask your students how they would interpret each of them."

She stopped and asked them right then. I especially liked the way one of the seniors paraphrased Matthew 5:40, which says:

> *If anyone wants to sue you and take your shirt,*
> *hand over your coat as well.*

The student's rendition? "You don't own anything anyway."

I just stared at the text, shaking my head and then read it aloud to myself:

> *You don't own anything anyway.*

He had nailed it. I thought about that one phrase over and over, and it reminded me of something outlandish that occurred with another friend.

Sharleen frequently opens her home. She is a kind and generous hostess; however, there was one particular guest who was causing her a bit of angst. The woman would come into Sharleen's house with roaming eyes. After a few moments she would point to an object, like a lamp, and say, "Sharleen, I really like this lamp. You should give it to me."

Sharleen would fill the awkwardness with a smile and a casual laugh. However, the same scenario repeated itself each and every time the woman came into her home, the only change being the article of the woman's coveting. *"Sharleen, I really like this chair. You should give it to me." "Sharleen, I really like these paper-mache giraffes. You should give them to me."*

Admittedly Sharleen was uncomfortable. But soon the discomfort turned into dread as she thought about the woman's next visit. Then the dread found a seed of bitterness. Sharleen didn't like how she was feeling towards this woman, so she did what Sharleen normally does: she went to the Lord, asking, "God, what do I do with this woman—she wants all my stuff!"

The reply came quickly: *"Give it to her."*

Sharleen is a woman who values God's whisperings, as well as her own peace and joy, much more than she did any belongings. She got the keys to her husband's pick-up truck, loaded every single coveted object into the truck and took it to the woman.

As the woman opened the door, she was surprised to see Sharleen. Sharleen tried to explain that she simply wanted to give all the items to her because she was becoming embittered.

As Sharleen told me later, "As I unloaded the stuff in her yard, I asked her to forgive me because I wasn't free to give it to her because all of it had a hold on me. She said that she wouldn't forgive me. I laughed and said, 'Well, that is between you and God.' And I drove away, free as a bird."

She didn't own anything anyway ... and neither do we.

Hot Chocolate

Often, in biblical times, the Roman soldiers ordered Jews, or other foreigners, to carry their heavy backpacks and equipment. It didn't matter if the Jew was going that way or not, he was required by law to carry it one mile and then return to where he started, thus two miles of walking. Time was lost, as was his plan for the day. It was mandatory to do to this, or the Jew would be flogged.

Jesus took the Roman demand and made a big leap, instructing them, *"Carry it an extra mile."*

An extra mile? That would mean two more miles, which would equal FOUR MILES of walking! Can you hear the gasps at this unreasonable request? Can you imagine the social media posts?

Most of us are content to do the bare minimum in order to check off the box. If an employer asks us to work late or a parent asks us to clean off the table, we become indignant. Inside we scream, *"I don't want to!"* or *"I don't have time."* We think, *"You should be pleased that I did anything at all."*

I must confess that I have struggled over this instruction to go the extra mile. But this is the Kingdom, and in the Kingdom, things are upside-down. So I asked God to give me His perspective.

Clearly, I heard, *"Karen, you GET to go the extra mile."* Oh.

In the Kingdom, going the extra mile is a privilege. And, in actually doing so, His Kingdom is revealed and realized. God never does the minimum for me. He always gives freely and generously. And He gives me the opportunity to do the same.

It was December. It was near freezing, and it was windy. I was dropping by the mall to run a quick errand. I pulled my hood up in a poor attempt to block the icy blasts as I hurried across the parking lot. As I approached the door, I heard the bell ringing, the first of this season's Salvation Army Red Kettle Bell Ringers.

I had long ago made a silent pledge to never pass by one of the ringers without dropping some money in their kettle. I smiled at the older gentleman and quickly said, "I'll be right back, and then I'll get ya!" He acknowledged my words as I scooted out of the wind and into the mall. It was then that I heard the familiar voice speak to my spirit, *"Get some hot chocolate for him on your way back."*

I ran my errand swiftly and stopped at the Cinnabon store as I headed to the door. The cashier asked for my order, and I said, "One medium hot chocolate."

"Would you like whipped cream with that?" I glanced at the menu to see upcharge: 35 cents.

"Naaahhh," I replied.

It was then I felt the jolt, almost like I was poked or like a mirror was suddenly flashed in my face and I saw how cruddy I really looked in that split second and how chintzy I appeared.

"YES!" I blurted out. "Yes, I'd like some whipped cream! And make it a large!"

It's the Kingdom. I get to go the extra mile.

How to Treat Others

The golden rule, *do to others as you would have them do to you*, is common and easy to quote. One translation puts it this way:

Ask yourself what you want people to do for you;
then grab the initiative and do it for them.
Matthew 7:12 MSG

Basically, treat other people the exact same way you want to be treated.

I know how I want to be treated. I want to be treated *good*, especially by family and friends, but also by strangers. I'd like it that way.

However, sometimes, on occasion, all of us simply forget the golden rule. We forget to treat others how we want to be treated. And that was the case with my friend, Tommy.

Tommy and his wife, Blanche, had been traveling in Brazil. One day they toured a place with a waterfall that could be walked under without getting wet. As they did so, they came across a one-legged man sitting behind a display of hand-carved wooden statues. As Tommy chatted with the man, he learned that the man himself was the artist. Tommy then sorted through all of the pieces until he found one that he wanted to take home and asked the man for the price. Tommy loves to barter and, after going back and forth, he finally was able to get the man down to fifteen US dollars, a good price for a hand-carved piece of art. Satisfied, Tommy paid the man and proudly carried away his treasure.

However, upon arriving back in the States and placing the unique carving in its new location in his home, a wave of disgust hit Tommy ... *what had he done?* The artist that he had met under the waterfall had not been begging; he was diligently working, day in and day out, to eke out a living in a poor country. Suddenly, Tommy was shockingly aware that he had beat down the man's asking price way below half of what he was originally asking for. Tommy was racked with shame and guilt.

It was then that Tommy did what Tommy knew to do. He asked God what he needed to do.

Though the timing was years later, Tommy handed me an envelope of cash. The cash, he said, was for me to use during my husband and my six-week sabbatical to South Africa. He explained that, though he knew this wouldn't help the man under the waterfall, he wanted to be able to bless others in similar conditions.

Tommy's request? Would I take the $500 and share it with as many one-legged men as I could find?

During our trip, I found several one legged men. They seemed to appear out of nowhere. Each and every time I'd ask God, *"How much?"* and eventually emptied my cash envelope.

But now that seed was planted in me. And since that time I have traveled to several parts of the world and God continues to bring one-legged men in my path. When I catch sight of them, I sense that familiar prompting, and I am able to, in some way, bless each one of them.

Tommy died a few months after his nintieth birthday. The story of the one-legged man under the waterfall was told at his funeral, a story that many of his family members were unaware of. Over and over I heard the same response, "I can't wait to bless a one-legged man ...."

Choosing to treat others how you want to be treated is definitely a way to find the Kingdom. And if you happen to, on occasion, do just the opposite the King still has a plan. He always has a plan.

Chapter Eight

Normal Everyday Stuff

There are simple things that each of us do everyday without even thinking—they are just routine. Things like considering where to park your car, acknowledging someone with eye contact or uttering a simple thank you to someone for opening a door is normal everyday stuff. So where do these small things fit in the Kingdom?

Consider the Ant

Open your eyes and there it is!
By taking a long and thoughtful look at what God
has created, people have always been able to see
what their eyes as such can't see: eternal power,
for instance, and the mystery of his divine being.
So nobody has a good excuse.
Romans 1:20 MSG

Each of us consider things all day, everyday. There is consideration of what I'm going to eat for lunch. I may consider whether I will use the elevator or the stairs. I might briefly consider if I will control my tongue or be a jerk. *Considering* something can result in a momentary choice: french fries or salad—or a more life-altering decision, like making a marriage proposal.

To *consider* means that I choose to think about something—to gaze steadily or reflectively, especially with regard to taking some action.

The Kingdom is all around us, and one way to seek it is to consider the stuff in it. Jesus told us to consider the lilies (or flowers) in the field:

> ... *Instead of looking at the fashions, walk out into the fields and look at the wildflowers. They never primp or shop, but have you ever seen color and design quite like it? The ten best-dressed men and women in the country look shabby alongside of them.*
> Matthew 6:28 MSG

Truly, considering the ant is a game-changer:

> *Look at an ant. Watch it closely;*
> *Let it teach you a thing or two. Nobody has to tell it*
> *what to do. All summer it stores up food;*
> *At harvest it stockpiles provisions.*
> Proverbs 6:6-8 MSG

Considering things invites God personally to show us the way that He does things in His Kingdom. If we considered *just an ant* or *just a lily* we would see and know more about God and the way He does things, thus finding the Kingdom. Anything can be considered. Anything!

George Washington Carver, one of my heroes, considered the peanut. There is a compelling anecdote about Carver praying: "Mr. Creator, show me the secrets of your universe." He was asking that God would reveal secrets to him about plants and vegetables.

As he retells the story, the reply from Heaven came back: "Little man, you're not big enough to know the secrets of My universe, but I'll show you the secret of the peanut." In the TrueNorth Quest Blog we learn that George Washington Carver gave himself to the "lowly peanut" and in doing so:

> ... *he identified several hundred elements in its seed and shell. As he put the elements together again in different forms, he uncovered over 300 uses for the peanut including various kinds of foods, oil, paint, ink, soap, shampoo, facial cream, plastics, and many other products.*

By considering what was right in front of him, Carver found the Kingdom and the rest of us are the beneficiaries!

The Nod

My husband bought a used Jeep. He had always wanted one and now he was the proud owner of the Jeep of his dreams.

One day as I was riding with him, I noticed something that he had never done before while driving any other vehicle. When another Jeep coming from the opposite direction rode past him, my husband would simply raise his index finger from the steering wheel and then nod to the driver. Simultaneously, the driver did the same thing to him. After seeing this happen a few times, I said to my husband, "what the heck?"

He explained that it was a Jeep thing—Jeep owners just acknowledged each other.

"What!? Like a club?" I teased. "Yes," he unaffectedly replied, "like a club."

And, indeed, it was club. I paid closer attention and it happened every time: a nod and a raised index finger. This acknowledgment thing was for real.

The first Bible verse I ever memorized was Proverbs 3:5-6:

Trust in the Lord with all think heart;
And lean not unto thine own understanding.
In all thy ways acknowledge him, and he shall
direct they paths.

Can you imagine what it would be like if acknowledging God was as intuitive as Jeep drivers acknowledging one another? What would it be like to just lift an index finger or give a nod to God—to just acknowledge that He is in the house?

A missionary friend writes about staying in the humble home of Papai Mafumo of South Africa. She notes, "I will never forget him waking at half past four in the mornings and saying to God: "Sawubona, Baba"—good morning, Father.

This little seed of a story impacted me so much that I, too, chose to begin each day by acknowledging God with, "Good morning, Father." Doing this is a small thing—almost too minor to mention. However, I recount it because the basic act of greeting God—choosing to acknowledge Him—opens doors in ways that cannot be described. It also keeps me from falling into the trap of "trying to be a good Christian"—if there was such thing!

Greeting God, speaking with Him, smiling at Him and even going to Him with a present angst is absolutely normal in the kingdom. Any way that we choose to acknowledge Him is connecting with the God of the universe who invites us to connect with Him!

Uh, Thank You

Five-year-old Robert made frequent visits to my back yard. He loved to watch the fish in my small goldfish pond. Robert was part of a triplet set and had lost one of his sisters in a tragic post-Christmas house fire only six months earlier. His family had moved into a house on our cul-de-sac. Whenever I saw him playing at the fish pond, I would meander back there to have a chat.

On this particular July day, my brief conversation with Robert forever tweaked my perspective of *thankfulness*.

Robert had a very thick southern drawl. As I strolled up, he casually spoke, noting the obvious. "It rained, Miss Karen."

"Yes, Robert, it did. God finally sent rain." We had been rain-less for weeks.

"We've been praying for rain a lot, haven't we?" he continued as he used his stick to slowly chase the goldfish.

"Yes, I am very thankful for it," I said as I looked at him with my hands on my hips, not being fully prepared for his five-year-old wisdom.

He continued in his slow, Alabama twang, "Did you *thank Him*?"

I stood still, stared at him and he stared back at me as he waited for my answer. I managed to grin slightly and replied honestly, "No. No, not yet. But I will now."

And I did. And I still do.

I have also thanked the now adult Robert, for planting a seed in my heart that dramatically moved me from a generic thankfulness, to actually *thanking Him*.

I often hear Robert's Alabama twang inside my head, *"did you thank Him?"* And when I do, I give God a nod, a glance, and a whisper, "Thank You ...."

Actually taking the time to thank God, to personally acknowledge the giver of all good things, is played out in what some of us consider to be a children's Bible story. The story of the healing of the ten lepers is extremely relevant. And the ending is where the Kingdom secret lies:

> *One of them [the lepers] when he realized that*
> *he was healed, turned around and came back,*
> *shouting his gratitude, glorifying God.*
> *He kneeled at Jesus' feet, so grateful.*
> *He couldn't thank him enough ....*
> Luke 17:14-16 MSG

This leper went from not only being healed on the outside from his leprosy but being healed on the inside as well. Purposing to thank the true Giver of life, made all the difference.

It seems simple, almost insignificant. Yet those glances, those small acts, usher in life.

Considering what God has made, acknowledging Him, and thanking Him—these things seem like no-brainers. However, they are all keys in the Kingdom—and keys open doors!

Chapter Nine

Finding the Kingdom

The obvious goal in seeking the Kingdom is to find it.

Psalm 119:91 clearly states that *all things* serve God. Since this is true, then the Kingdom can be found *anywhere* and in *anything*. I really can't say it enough: wherever my feet are is a good place to seek the Kingdom.

Also, while seeking the Kingdom I adopted a rather simple, childlike view of this quest and was energized to find this:

Unless you return to square one and start over like children, you're not even going to get a look at the kingdom, let anyone get in. Whoever becomes simple and elemental again like this child will rank high in God's kingdom.
Matthew 18: 3-4 MSG

Sometimes I *purpose to look* for His Kingdom. Other times God sort of knocks me in the head with it. Following are just a few examples of finding the Kingdom in some odd ways and interesting places.

Piper

As I sat at a round table filled with other chatty women, my eye caught sight of Piper coming in the back door from the playground. Piper was an adorable seven-year-old girl who was the picture of precociousness. It was quite easy for her to engage in conversations with adults by asking questions and listening to their replies. She enjoyed the attention, and the adults enjoyed the interaction.

On this particular evening, she looked very distraught. Her coat was half on one shoulder, with the other half dragging on the floor as she haphazardly limped into the room.

Piper has a tendency to magnify whatever particular plight she finds herself in, so seeing her like this wasn't unusual. I called her over, "Piper, what's wrong, sweetie?"

She dropped her head to the side and in a rather dramatic fashion whimpered, "I've lost my shoe." Sure enough, I looked at her feet, only to see one shoe. She did have two socks. Whew.

"Well, Piper, where'd you last see your missing shoe?" I asked.

She swung her free arm to the side door, leading to the corridor and proclaimed, "In my classroom, I think ...."

"Then why were you looking for it outside?" I questioned.

She had a few whimpers left in her, but no concrete answers, so I made a brilliant suggestion. "Piper, why don't you go look for your shoe in the classroom, since that is the last place you saw it?"

It was then that I felt that highlight, the instinct to pause, that says, *"Pay attention! Selah!"*

As she limped away towards her classroom, the still quiet Voice whispered: *"Pay attention to this: when you lose something that I have promised to you, go to the last place you saw it in order to get it back."*

Losing My Shoe

*... the kingdom of God is not eating
and drinking, but righteousness and peace
and joy in the Holy Spirit.*
Romans 14:17 NIV

I flew to Antigua, Guatemala in order to meet up with the group that I was coaching for their final debrief. I was excited about seeing the young adults that I had invested in for the last eleven months.

Casual conversation ruled the breakfast table on our first morning as the small leadership team met. Out of my mouth came, in retrospect, a very surprising question:

"So, what do y'all think of Kaepernick kneeling during the NFL games?"

I quickly noticed the slightly perplexed reactions and began to feel uneasy. No one replied; they just shrugged their shoulders and looked down at their plates. I put my question in my back pocket and changed the subject.

It was at that very moment that I had the realization: I had *lost my shoe.*

Yup, both peace and joy were gone. My two markers—actually everyone's two markers—for walking in the Kingdom had both slipped away. I was totally flat. The realization of this wasn't evident until the awkwardness at the table had appeared, but now there was nothing hidden.

I went back to my room and put on praise music. I had a pure motive. I wanted to connect with God in order to get my peace and joy back, but learned a lesson within a lesson: worshiping the God of the universe is definitely a key to the Kingdom. However, simply putting on praise music does not necessarily mean that He is actually being worshiped.

It felt eerily like I was attempting to conjure up peace and joy or, dare I say it, manipulate God. There was nothing—no peace, no joy. I was now restless, on top of feeling embarrassed. It was one of my last meetings with my leadership team, and I had brought up politics of all things. *Ugh.*

I went through my day pondering and asking—OK, *begging*—God to help me find where I had lost my joy and peace! Was it sin? I simply couldn't figure it out. All I knew for certain was that both were gone.

That evening, a handful of people on the team went out for supper. As we were gathering our money to pay for the pizza, I heard Him clearly speak: *"It's the book you are reading."*

My jaw dropped as I mouthed the word: *"Really?"* I knew in an instant what had happened.

Months earlier, with the desire to be an informed voter, I had begun reading several political books, the most recent being a very dicey tale. The political kingdom had definitely enticed me.

"God, what do You want me to do?" I had long ago learned that with God, there is almost always some point of obedience when in retrieval mode, and I desperately wanted to retrieve my peace and joy.

Clearly, I heard, *"Delete it off your Kindle."*

I couldn't get back to my room quick enough. I flung open the door, ran to my bedside table and picked up the Kindle: delete! The volatile political culture had ensnared me, but now, after a simple act of obedience, I was unfettered. Then, quicker than my book disappeared into cyberspace, my peace and my joy returned.

It had been too easy to stop seeking the Kingdom *first*. The subtle shift from seeking the Kingdom to seeking other kingdoms was notable.

To this day I have to purpose not to fill my mind with the political stuff. I can always tell when I have read or watched or listened to too much, because of the absence of the two internal Kingdom markers: peace and joy.

Seek first his kingdom and his righteousness,
and all these things will be given to you as well.
Matthew 6:33 KJV

Chapter Ten

Finding Kingdom in Music

When I was a teenager in the 1970s, I heard about the horrors of rock 'n roll from more than one well-meaning Christian speaker. Each had their list of reasons for urging all the teenagers in the room to avoid listening to it. Most of these speakers had been set free from its noted destructive tentacles.

Though my head and heart couldn't reconcile this uncompromising sentiment, I eventually made the choice to avoid listening to any secular music, especially rock 'n roll.

This borrowed conviction made its way into my parenting. As my three sons were growing up, I made the conscious choice to allow them to listen only to Christian music. However, my husband, who has never been one to ever borrow anyone's convictions—even his dear wife's—had his car radio set on 95.1, a classic rock station. This, of course, threw a minor wrench in my personal parenting system, which I simply chose to over look.

In retrospect, I chose wisely to ignore his choice and he chose wisely to ignore mine.

Therefore, my sons grew accustomed to DC Talk, Audio Adrenalin, Jars of Clay and David Crowder while in my vehicle, and classic rock 'n roll while in my husband's. I purposed to gather as many tape cassettes as they could possibly desire since I was filling their heads with good things. Though this sounds like a noble course, I was totally missing so many golden opportunities to seek the Kingdom, as well as teach them how to seek the Kingdom, while they lived under my roof—and rode in my car!

I can still recall the day that my first born, the first one through the mom gauntlet, asked if he could listen to the Dave Matthew's Band. *Permission granted* since he had earned lots of trust over the years. That was the beginning of the end of my edict. All three of my sons ventured into music that I would have never chosen for them to listen to. Or so, I thought.

My then fifteen-year-old son is now in his thirties. During those fifteen-plus years, I listened to Dave Matthews enough to know many of the lyrics to several of his songs. I made a little life-altering discovery: The Kingdom can even be found in music. After all, *all things serve God.*

My journey with God and the entire kingdom of music (with it's many sub-kingdoms) has been long, and at times arduous. For instance, several years ago, I chose to take a hiatus from listening to Christian music. My decision came after considering many factors, the first being that too many of the popular trendy Christian songs that were finding their way to my streaming music shuffle sounded cliché and trite. I found myself pushing the thumbs-down button way too often.

I left it all. I made the decision, like Julia Robert's character in the movie *Runaway Bride,* to figure out how I liked my eggs cooked.

I discovered that I do indeed have my own personal likes and dislikes. I have even honed several playlists that are uniquely mine. In doing so, I found that I was actually *hearing* a few songs that I had only heard in public places, which meant that I was finally understanding the actual lyrics.

Many of these lyrics had something I had not expected: Kingdom.

One of the very first that stood out to me was OneRepublic's "Something I Need."

Hidden in the middle of the first verse is a great lyric that lines up with the way God does things in His Kingdom:

But you're like the net under the ledge
When I go flying off the edge,
you go flying off as well

Though I have repeatedly heard that God would catch me when I fall, I was continually baffled when He let me fall flat on my face. However, He does promise that He will always be with me and will never leave me nor turn His back on me.

This was amazing. I listened to the song over and over and found more Kingdom in the refrain of the same song:

You got something I need
In this world full of people there's one killing me
And if we only die once
I wanna die with you

In the Kingdom, God wants us to die to ourselves. That is the way it is in His Kingdom. *Less of me, more of Him* is the way to life. I have personally discovered over the years that there is indeed more life when there is less of me.

But the last line of the song totally captured me:

If we only live once
I wanna live with you.

In this Kingdom ruled by a sovereign King, He always gives us a choice. The ultimate choice is how will I live? Since I get to choose, I want to live with Him.

The more I listened to the extreme amount of genres and songs; the more overwhelmed I became. Finding the Kingdom in music was like finding buds on a tree in the spring. The amount of life-giving and truth-filled lyrics piqued my curiosity and actually confirmed that truly *all things serve Him.*

Yes, I found and still find a lot of junk, but isn't the ability to search through whatever and find gold actually the point of *seeking*?

I also discovered that the writer of the song doesn't necessarily even have to know that he or she is exposing the Kingdom. They could have strategically written the song that way, or been totally unaware of the gold.

The Kingdom can be found throughout a whole song or maybe in just one line or lyric. It can be as simple as hearing a snippet of a conversation between God and Satan, God and a person, Satan and person, or finding a line about *the way* He does things.

I was, and am, definitely *finding*. Lots. So I finally made a playlist labeled, "Finding Kingdom." To this day, finding the kingdom in songs has become easy, and almost second nature.

Sam

*Music expresses that which cannot be said
and on which it is impossible to be silent.*

—Victor Hugo

Presenting the concepts of the Kingdom to a group is always challenging. It is similar to attempting to explain the game of football to someone during the final minutes of the Super Bowl—so many nuances in the middle of so much activity. It's just too much. It's best to start small.

One way to tell others about the Kingdom is through music. Music has strange powers. Certain instruments can beckon to be picked up after years of neglect or stir up reminders of a past experience. A song can take us back in time. It has the potential to reduce us to tears or to make our spirits soar. One song can ruin a perfectly beautiful evening or motivate a team to victory. Songs help us grieve, celebrate, calm down, or work more efficiently. Music has power. All music, ultimately, serves God.

When I learned to seek the Kingdom in music, I found a way to inspire individuals to discover Kingdom on their own. In teaching sessions about my own discoveries, they were encouraged to find the kingdom in their favorite music. This enabled them to start small.

During one teaching session, I mentioned that my two least favorite genres of music were country and rap. I heard the groans, but that didn't faze me.

Until I met Sam.

Sam approached me after the meeting and said he was okay with everything I had said except for my aversion to rap music. I shrugged my shoulders. I cared not.

He went onto say, "But I love the teaching." We both smiled. We were back on level ground.

"But I do have a question," he began, "I know that I have found the Kingdom in rap music." I nodded. "But, what do you think about all the cussing ...?"

A trap? I think not.

"Well," I began slowly, trying hard to measure my words. Sam was big, like football-player-big, but in a teddy bear kind of way, like he could hug you and choose to crush you if he wished.

I continued, "Don't tell anyone I said this, because I doubt many would approve, but I think that the cussing is just one way to keep the religious away from those songs and it is also a way for some people who would never see the Kingdom otherwise to be exposed to it."

Sam audibly exhaled, stepped back, and smiled a large and powerful smile. Relief took over him. He was at the precipice and wanted to jump, but from my perspective, he wanted to make sure that the kingdom that he was interested in could experience His Kingdom coming. It can! It does!

Sam asked if I would give a few songs a listen.

"Sure! Why not!?"

I did. Since that time Sam and I have exchanged a few emails discussing how we've found the Kingdom in those songs. Rap is still not my cup of tea, however, I can definitely see the Kingdom in it.

Everything is Everything

Since all things serve God, then music is just one place to find the obvious gold mines of Kingdom. Kingdom can be found in movies, plays, television shows, commercials, concerts, art, paintings, conversations, books, and so much more.

Obviously, the list could go on and on, and it does. Here is an email from a young woman who had heard my teaching on finding the Kingdom in music. She took it a little further and found the Kingdom on the highway.

Hi Karen,

My name is Dara ... I loved your seeking kingdom session! Ever since then I've seen so much more kingdom, I have done the song thing for a long time but never put it in those terms before and I feel like I do it even more now!

I drove in from Texas with a couple of squadmates, and the Lord convicted me of my speeding. I speed a lot. And so I was being obedient and driving the speed limit, God showed me so much kingdom while I was driving!

Like how when we can get focused on those around us and start going with the flow, going their speed because everyone else is going that pace, and we look down, and we are going like 15 over the speed limit! Let me tell you, Alabama has a speeding problem!

In the construction zones, it would be 55 and people would fly past me going 80, I noticed myself having white knuckles as people passed me (big pet peeve) and yet I just continued to go the speed limit. I found my anxiety went down because I wasn't on the lookout for cops, trying not to get caught for speeding. I enjoyed the drive more once I let loose of the steering wheel a little and gave up the race of the other cars. The cruise control became my best friend, because once it was set to the correct speed, I didn't have to worry, like the Holy Spirit, once you trust your pace with God and let the Holy Spirit lead you it becomes easier.

I also noticed that I paid more attention to the signs so that if I got the chance to go faster, I wouldn't miss it. It's like in life, when we are actively waiting for God and sticking to His pace and not ours, and then He gives us a sign, an opportunity to grow or provision or the next step we get to go a little faster or sometimes a little slower.

It was also really humbling when semi after semi just kept passing me, and yet after a while, I felt so much joy because I was being obedient and driving with Jesus. God showed me that in life I will see others "moving faster" maybe in their walk with Him or moving further along in life with status, money, or their job, but I need to trust in the pace and growth God is moving in me and trust His plan over mine.

I was thrilled to get this email. The Kingdom seeds I had thrown out fell on good soil. Yes, she had been seeking the Kingdom all along, she just had not put it in those terms. Knowing that gold is gold is a fairly phenomenal thing!

Everything is everything, every single day.

"I Believe" Michael Franti

Part Three

Life in the Kingdom

Chapter Eleven

A Kingdom Worth Dying For

Aly and I walked down a wooded path, very aware that we only had two hours to catch up on our live's happenings. What began as a very casual chat grew serious as Aly repeated what God had been telling her. It was a simple phrase but one that she was hearing over and over: *"Aly, that's not yours."*

"Yep, that sounds like God," I replied.

She smiled that smile. It is the smile that I love seeing more than any other facial expression while chatting with people. It is the smile that says, *"I am getting it. I am understanding how to walk with Him in the Kingdom."*

Denying yourself is more than simply saying "no" to ice cream or a joint or porn. That type of denying yourself reflects a rather small understanding of the Kingdom and the King.

Jesus Himself taught us how to deny ourselves by denying Himself. He modeled it, but more than that, He enables us actually to do it, from the inside out.

Denying yourself, or rather, putting others before yourself is the realization that the time that our feet have on this planet is short. It is an understanding that I own nothing, yet I possess everything.

Giving up my rights, my dreams, my wants, my plans, my passions, my hopes, my everything, means that, in actuality, I end up with more.

That, in a nutshell, is faith.

So what does God want from me? Jesus says it this way:

Simply put, if you're not willing to take what is dearest to you, whether plans or people, and kiss it good-bye, you can't be my disciple.
Luke 14:33 MSG

Me First?

There is an old Monty Python movie, set in medieval times, where a town employee is walking up and down the cobblestone streets pushing a large wooden wheelbarrow stacked full of dead bodies due to the plague.

As he walks, the employee continually calls out, "Bring out your dead," and it becomes painfully obvious that he oversees the collection of newly dead bodies. One of the townspeople comes out to the body collector with a frail old man thrown over his shoulder and attempts to put him into the already full wheelbarrow.

Suddenly, the presumably dead old man weakly proclaims, "I'm not dead!" The response is quick and curt from the gentleman carrying him. "Yes, you are."

"I'm not dead," comes the feeble reply. The gentleman ignores him and attempts to give the body collector the nine pence to take the man. The body collector, in a rather righteous moment, says, "He says he's not dead."

"He is."

"He says he isn't."

"He isn't?"

"I'm not," chimes in the old man.

"Well, he will be soon. He's very ill."

"I'm getting better."

"No, you're not. You'll be stone dead in a moment."

The tense argument continues. The gentleman wants the old man gone and fretfully asks the body collector, "Isn't there something you can do?"

The collector glances around and then comes up with a solution. He steps towards the old man and bops him on the head with a blunt object, rendering him quite dead.

The town employee collects his nine pence, the supposed friend plops the newly dead man into the cart, and the transition is complete. Life goes on as normal ... except for the newly dead, that is.

God wants me dead.

God wants me dead, and I have even said aloud that I want to be dead: *"less* of me, more of You." Do I even have an inkling of the ramifications of that short statement which so casually rolled off my tongue?

It sounds rather gallant (brave, courageous, heroic, fearless) to pray such a prayer, to make such a proclamation. That is until He begins to render me dead, that is, until He starts to eke away at the very person He created—until He tears at my flesh and crushes my soul. It's all fun and games until the very favor that once drew people towards me begins to wane, leaving me and some points ignored, even despised.

Until there is substantially less of me.

I tend to respond to my angst, large or small, by rebuking the devil and his cohorts to no avail.

I scream to God, "WHERE ARE YOU?" only to be answered with stale air and another push under the water.

"I'm dying!" I scream in panic, and the only thing I hear is a faint whisper simply suggesting, like Sara Bareilles does in her "Love Song" that I, "breathe easy for a while."

He reminds me that I had actually asked for this when I mumbled my prayer, *"Less of me, more of You."*

It *feels* awful.

It *is* awful until I heed His prompting—simply to breathe, which just happens to be my only role at this juncture.

The physical affects the spiritual which affects the emotional which affects the physical. The mind, the body, the soul, the spirit all seemingly combat one another, but the Spirit is the One that needs to win this battle of wills. His Spirit, intertwined with mine, causes the battle to wane. *He is alive in me.*

I am more careful now about what I pray, what I ask for, what I sing, what I proclaim. The Kingdom, His Kingdom, often baffles me. I get confused, but I always, always know the truth that He has eternity in mind. My most major role is to trust Him.

Now, more often than not, I choose simply to be silent in His presence. He continues to do an amazing job of putting His finger to my lips as a reminder not to open my mouth too quickly in confessing the obvious fact that "I'm not dead ...." He already knows and has let me know over and over that this Kingdom, is indeed, worth dying for.

Less of me. More of You. Those six words. Oh, those six words.

If we only live once, I wanna live with you.

"Something I Need" by One Republic

Chapter Twelve

Entering the Kingdom

You can't love the kingdoms of this world in all their impressive, yet temporary, splendor *and* also love God's eternal Kingdom. It's impossible. No one can serve two masters. You will either love one and hate the other or hate one and love the other.

Each of us, every one of us that He created, *gets* to make the choice. He *first* chose us, all of us, and then gives us the opportunity to choose to either receive or reject Him and His Kingdom. In other words, one way or another, I will be choosing to turn my back on one kingdom in order to fully embrace another.

When I was single, I acted like a single lady. I made choices based on me and me alone. I went where I wanted, when I wanted. I did what I wanted to do. I flirted with whom I wanted to flirt. I stayed up all night long if I felt like it. I wore my family's name proudly.

In August 1983, I accepted an invitation to become a married lady. In accepting that invitation, I was choosing to leave the single life behind and all that went with it. I chose to turn my back on the way I did things, and I embraced this man and our new married life. I chose to fully bear this new name, his name, and all that came with it.

On May 26, 1984, I began that new life. I began making decisions differently: I made them *with* someone, rather than making them alone. Old things were passed away and behold, all things were new.

Yes, I felt the same, looked the same, physically talked and walked the same. However, I was different! I had been transferred from the *kingdom of singleness* into the *kingdom of marriage*. The invitation was offered, and I made my choice. I would no longer live the way a single lady lives. I had a new way of living.

How to Enter the Kingdom

Bottom line is, the King loves us. All of us. He never turns up His nose to anyone that He created. Never. There is no sin that He cannot or will not forgive. He simply wants us to come to Him *just the way we are*, with a contrite (apologetic, humble, remorseful, repentant) heart and open hands.

But let's start at the beginning.

When God created everything, He placed us humans, the crown of His creation, on a wonderland planet where we walked with Him and enjoyed Him. He also gave us the ability to choose. The ultimate choice for each of us was and still is, to reject or embrace Him and His ways.

Adam and Eve, the first humans, chose their own way, thus really screwing up all of our futures. Read Genesis 1-3; it's heavy stuff. Basically, we all became dead, much like the zombies on the *Walking Dead* television show—decaying bodies with dead spirits.

However, I can't wholly blame them for my state. I, too, have been given the choice several times to choose God's way or my way. I, like Adam and Eve, have chosen my own way, therefore, affirming my own personal *deadness*.

Choosing my way over my Creator's way is called sin. It is my sin that keeps me from God and from enjoying God as well as fully enjoying the life that He intended for us as humans to live.

In order to protect us from ourselves, God set up laws. Man has taken liberty with these laws over the last several thousand years and embellished them, therefore making God seemingly *religious*, rather than personal—so many laws that are impossible to keep.

However, when the time was right, this loving God sent Jesus, His only Son, who lived a perfect life and became the perfect sacrifice (or rather He received the punishment) for my sin. He died in my place.

Three days after He died, God reached down and in some crazy God way, touched Him, bringing Jesus back to life again. At that second, the very power of sin and death was crushed.

Then, the God of Abraham, Isaac, and Jacob, did what no other god does: He gave, and still gives, all of us an invitation to simply *believe* what He has done for us in order to walk with Him again. Jesus puts it this way:

Anyone here who believes what I am saying
right now and aligns himself with the Father,
who has, in fact, put me in charge,
has at this very moment the real, lasting life
and is no longer condemned to be an outsider.
This person has taken a giant step from the
world of the dead to the world of the living.
John 5:24 MSG

Believing, like Jesus said, means that you believe the King loves you, wants to be in a relationship with you and that you are ready and willing to put Him in charge of *everything* that defines you!

Surrender is the ultimate act of trust.

Surrender means that you don't straddle the fence. Surrender means you choose a side and jump. Surrender means you open your hands and let go. Surrender means you give up your sword, your fight. You burn your ships; there is no going back. Surrender means that He, Himself and His Kingdom *is it*.

It seems that all my bridges have been burned
But you say "That's exactly how this grace thing works."
It's not the long walk home that will change this heart
But the welcome I receive with every start.

"Roll Away Your Stone" by Mumford and Sons

When you first believe, you are automatically transferred from the Kingdom of Darkness into God's Kingdom. With that decision, the Holy Spirit, because you have welcomed Him, comes to live inside of you. Your once dead spirit is now brought to life. Your sin? Eradicated.

God rescued us from dead-end alleys
and dark dungeons. He's set us up in the Kingdom
of the Son He loves so much, the Son who got us
out of the pit we were in, got rid of the sins we
were doomed to keep repeating.
Colossians 1:13-14 MSG

It is at this point, the point when you know that your life is not your own, that you now belong fully to God. Putting yourself, your very life, in His hands is *trust*.

He is the King, and you get to follow Him today (and the next day and the next day and ...). Obeying Him is how you walk in this crazy Kingdom. Obedience to God is the ultimate key to the Kingdom.

Chapter Thirteen

Walking in the Kingdom

Kingdom is where the abundant life that Jesus mentioned exists. Learning to seek it is paramount. Choosing to walk in it consciously creates a brand new anticipation of each and every day. Paul says it this way:

> *So here's what I want you to do, God helping you: Take your everyday, ordinary life—your sleeping, eating, going-to-work, and walking-around life and place it before God as an offering. Embracing what God does for you is the best thing you can do for him.*
> Romans 12:1 MSG

Today

Purposing to live fully in *today* is one of the keys of the Kingdom.

This day, today, is the day God has made. It is the very day that He wants us to experience, to embrace, to live in. The majority of people that I know do not live in today. They are either constantly looking backward or worrying about tomorrow.

Jesus talks about yesterday like this:

No man, having put his hand to the plow,
and looking back, is fit for the kingdom of God.
Luke 9:62 KJV

When plowing ground, it is essential to keep your eyes on the end of the desired row that you are creating. If you get distracted, the straight line will stray either to the left or the right. If you look backward, you may find yourself plowing a circle.

Yesterday could have been full of grief, self-centeredness, or deep regrets. Or it could have been full of youthfulness, glitz, or popularity. All of these things have one thing in common, though: they are in the past. The Message translation puts Luke 9:62 this way:

No procrastination. No backward looks.
You can't put God's kingdom off till tomorrow.
Seize the day.

Looking backward breeds, what my husband calls, *navel-gazing.* Navel-gazing literally means staring at your own belly button. Figuratively, it means that you are focused only on yourself.

Focusing on your past likely means that you are wishing for a re-do. The *I shouldas* and the *I couldas* will suck the very life out of you.

Worrying about tomorrow is also fairly easy. Heck, worrying is fairly easy! Worrying is focusing on something that you can do nothing about. Some people have crafted the ability to worry, going so far to even making world events their responsibility.

Jesus has a lot to say about worrying, which He sums up concisely:

> *Don't worry about tomorrow,*
> *for tomorrow will bring its own worries.*
> *Today's trouble is enough for today.*
> Matthew 6:35 NLT

He knows we have trouble in today, trouble that may affect tomorrow, but today really does have enough stuff to be concerned about. This isn't simply good or trite advice. *Today* is the day we are to be camping out, not tomorrow, nor yesterday.

It is easy to learn the skill of worrying, but not so easy to unlearn it, which is why we have a King. Throwing all that stuff at Him is also a learned skill. It is saying, in essence, "I don't want to worry, so here!"

When I give Him something, the inside of my head has to go somewhere. Emptiness is not an option:

> *Seek ye first the kingdom of God, and his*
> *righteousness; and all these things*
> *shall be added unto you.*
> Matthew 6:33 KJV

Just start small, today.

The Banqueting Table

He brought me to the banqueting table,
His banner over me is love ....

"His Banner Over Me" by Kevin Prosch

We sang the song in the 1970s, but like the lyrics of many songs, the meaning has been lost.

The banqueting table had its first mention in the Old Testament. Unfortunately, it seems to have been added to the list of seemingly ethereal things that occur after we die. The truth is that the banqueting table is what God lays before each of us daily after sprinkling it with the option to choose.

I get to choose.

Tammy is one of my best friends on the planet. She is also a caterer. For my husband's 50th birthday she made all of his favorite dishes and displayed them on our ping-pong table which she beautifully re-purposed as a banqueting table. It was stunning.

Tim's eyes widened as he walked around the table: watermelon, fresh veggies, breads, and a variety of sweets and meats. Tim was in disbelief but managed to say, "I don't know where to start." Tammy smiled. She knew she had succeeded in providing an overabundance of choices for him and his guests.

She had saved her biggest surprise for last. She pointed towards the corner of the table and said, "Go over there." Tim walked around to the other side, to the corner, and lifted the lid of the serving dish: bacon wrapped scallops ... his ultimate favorite!

She wasn't going to let him miss out on a thing!

Way too often we have a fear of missing God and what some call, "His best." Because of this fear we tend to get distracted from the Kingdom, or we begin fantasizing about the life we "should have" or we simply freeze and do nothing. Today can slip by by when we simply wait for the elusive job offer or for the person of our dreams to suddenly appear and rescue us from our present misery.

Note: If God specifically says, "*wait*," then, obviously, we wait. Active waiting may mean staying in a certain town when wanting to move while knowing that He was said, "stay put." Waiting, when He tells you to do it, is active obedience. Waiting can be our role.

Often when we pray, however, the answer is right there. If we open our spiritual eyes we could clearly see the banqueting table that He has prepared while saying, "*You choose.*"

You walked around and you planted seeds,
your kingdom came up from among the weeds
and the men all cried while staring at the trees
saying, "what are we supposed to see?"
Well, I say you'll see freedom.
Stop looking at the ground,
start looking at the leaves
Up among the dirt and rust
is where the kingdom breathes
You'll see freedom.

"The Gown of Green" by The Collection

Choosing is a simple task. However, some wonder, "If I eat the croissant will I miss the bacon-wrapped scallops?" No! The amazing thing is, God doesn't set the table and then walk away. He promises us that He will lead and guide us, and He does, even during the very process of our choosing. He is quite able to beckon us to wherever He wants us to be. After all, He is God.

In choosing at this banqueting table, it is vital to know that all choices have results or consequences and, to quote a great man that I happened to be married to, "The small choices make the big choices."

For instance, getting up early is a good thing especially if you have obligations. If you have a day off, then choosing to sleep till 11:00 might be a good thing. It is, after all, your choice. However, in choosing those extra hours of sleep, you may miss hiking with friends. Yet, in staying home, you may have gained rest. No one can make the small choices for another person. We each make them daily, many times. All of them have results. Choosing is always better than not choosing.

I have talked to many, many twenty-somethings who are waiting for life to happen to them. They live their entire lives thinking that tomorrow is going to be when the nebulous *it* happens.

One adventurous young lady once said to me, "I want to travel." I asked, "Do you have your passport?" She replied, "No, because I don't have the money to travel." I respond, "Do you do things around here, like hike?"

"No," she replied, "I really want to go to Europe." I countered, "I don't want to hear it." She seemed surprised, yet I continued, "You say you want to travel, yet you don't have your passport and you aren't willing to start exploring what is right in front of you. The opportunity to travel overseas will more than likely happen, but, first, open your eyes to the free things to do that are right in front of you."

Today, this same young lady's Instagram is marked by her ongoing and frequent adventures. She also has her passport and an overseas trip planned. The small choices made the big choices.

Today is the day the King wants us to fully live. Looking backward causes crooked lines, or worse, stagnation. Borrowing tomorrow via worrying or fantasizing is a diversion from the life God created us to live. However, taking the time to consider my life in the context of today and what today has to offer is a tremendous way to start small.

Today is a key to the Kingdom.

You will have complete and free access to God's
kingdom, keys to open any and every door:
no more barriers between heaven and earth,
earth and heaven. A yes on earth is yes in heaven.
A no on earth is no in heaven.
Matthew 16:19 MSG

Whaddaya Got?

God blessed them, and God said unto them,
Be fruitful, and multiply, and replenish
the earth and subdue it...
Genesis 1:28 KJV

Planet earth is the wonderland which God bids us to subdue—bring under control—while walking in His amazing non-religious Kingdom. This grand God, with His own upside-down way of doing things, invites us to participate on a large scale by starting small right now, with whatever we have access to and with whoever is right in front of us at any given time.

Starting small as we walk on this planet means to note what is right at our fingertips.

Jesus tells the story of the widow who had earlier that day assessed what she had. She had two coins and made the choice to give those small coins, unashamedly, at the same time that the big bucks were being dropped into the temple treasury. Jesus noticed the reality of what was, in Kingdom terms, a transaction, rather than a donation:

> *This poor widow has put in more than all the others. All these people gave their gifts out of their wealth, but she out of her poverty put in all she had to live on.*
> Luke 21:3-4 NIV

Looking at what you have with Kingdom eyes—even if what you have is the least—alters reality and the unseen realm takes note.

Our group arrived in New Orleans within a year of Hurricane Katrina's devastation. We came to help—to cut grass, to hammer nails, to encourage local residents, and basically to do whatever was needed. When we arrived, we found the expected overgrown yards, ravaged homes, and abandoned businesses.

What we didn't expect was the condition of the residents who had remained in the devastation. They had a desire—a need—to talk. So many of them wanted to share the personal details of their specific circumstances, in the midst of everyone's general misery.

Their homes were destroyed, their jobs had disappeared, and many, if not most, were suddenly and inadvertently dependent on government help. This help amounted to the provision of temporary metal containers that they now called home. They saw no foreseeable possibility of rebuilding what was lost.

Most of the people that we encountered had sad eyes and peeling hands—sad eyes because their lives were now so stagnant; peeling hands because of the bleach they used to scrub the continually encroaching mold and mildew. They wondered aloud whether they should cut their losses and leave, or continue in the uncertainty.

One day, while our group was setting up for a makeshift vacation Bible school for the local children, a middle-aged man, one of the local church members, walked into the building. He was wearing a grin and carrying a small shopping bag.

Very meticulously, he worked his way around the room. As he moved from person to person, he would reach into his bag and pull out one of the small objects therein, placing it in the hand of the volunteer in front of him.

He eventually made his way to me, and I was the last one to receive one of the mystery gifts. I held out my hand as he placed a hand-painted rock into my hand.

"This is for you," he said with a grin.

I smiled my most gracious smile and quickly examined my rock. It was a just a bit larger than an egg, quite smooth, and had been clumsily painted with blue, green, and yellow paint.

As I turned it over, I noted that the name, "Jesus" had been hand-lettered on one side of it.

"Oh," I said. "How nice."

In my head, the thought came, *"What am I going to do with a painted rock?"*

Being sincerely curious, though, I said to the kind gentleman, "Tell me about this ...."

He seemed glad that I asked, and replied, "Everyone here is so sad. So I asked God what I could do to help. I looked around, and I had rocks, and I had paint. He told me to paint these rocks and give them to everyone to encourage them. It's the least I could do."

It is the least I could do.

The least will be the greatest.

This gentleman had sought the Kingdom and then found it, though he might not have put it in those terms. His prayer had been simple, but he had a yes in his heart. God had provided what he needed in order to obey.

With his whole heart, he offered his gifts to us, to me.

I still have my rock. It's a constant reminder of the importance of one person choosing to start small by assessing and subduing what was in front of him: paint and rocks. Was this any different than the widow giving all she had?

Subduing the earth is a hefty assignment. An assignment that the large majority of humankind has simply overlooked. Yes, there are many people who are subduing different aspects of this planet, but many are clueless that we even have this assignment. Then there are the few that are choosing to start small, in their tiny part of the Kingdom.

They are assessing what they have and doing what the King puts in their heart.

Great gifts mean great responsibilities;
greater gifts, greater responsibilities!
Luke 12:48 MSG

Chapter Fourteen

A Gnat's Breath Away

I like clear warnings, especially when others have walked a path before me.

Here is a little warning and it is applicable to any serious believer who chooses to seek the Kingdom above all else. These following things happen subtly, but, unfortunately, they do happen.

Each of us, upon choosing to walk in the Kingdom, is a gnat's breath away from being *religious, complacent,* or *cynical.*

A gnat's breath is a good ol' Southern expression meaning a split-second of time.

Religion

My personal definition of *religion,* in the context of Christianity, is *going through the motions without any apparent need of God Himself.* It is creating a personally manageable system that looks good and even feels right, but it is void of His life.

In other words, a beautiful, meaningful connection with God one day can turn religious when attempting to recreate it. Doing that over and over gives oneself over to religion.

Over the years God has led me to pray specific prayers over specific individuals. Those prayers felt Spirit-led and life-filled. Then there are times I chose to just fill empty or awkward space by praying general, generic and wordy prayers over the person in front of me. Both prayers may have had similar words; however, in actuality, one was perfunctory, and therefore, religious.

This can get dicey especially when someone is asking you to pray for them right then and there. At one of our training camps, a young lady asked my husband to pray for her. He knew in his knower that he was not supposed to do so at that moment. So, much to her surprise, he said, "No." Later, however, God did prompt him with a specific prayer for her. Though his initial response totally confused her, she clearly saw the broader picture later because of his obedience.

The line between religion and life can be blurry, but a true follower knows the sound of His voice. The King is able to provide a prayer to pray in an instant, and it is a good thing to wait on Him. Praying an obligatory, time-filling prayer can be religious.

Early in my married life, I established a morning time ritual where I did my Bible reading and clicked through a very long prayer list. Sometimes it took 20 minutes, sometimes an hour and a half, but I was consistent, until the morning that I closed my Bible and started to get up from my chair and heard in my spirit, *"You didn't even say, 'Hi.'"*

My relationship with God had turned religious, but quickly turned back into a relationship. It was, and is, too easy to veer towards religion. Fortunately, God allows me to regroup a lot.

Complacent

My personal definition of *complacent* is *bored, marked by a dramatically waning care-meter.*

For believers, this occurs when our focus shifts from God and others onto me (my issues, my past, my dreams, my future, my successes—or lack thereof) or onto my ministry (what I am doing or not doing.) It also occurs when there is an absence of challenge.

We have acquaintances who live in Uganda, but they started out in South Korea. The husband, Daniel, was a co-pastor at a large, thriving church in South Korea. He and his wife, Eunice, admittedly were becoming complacent. The church was doing well, but they weren't personally challenged—they were *gliding.*

It was at that juncture that they did the right next thing: they asked God what to do.

God always has something for us to do in the Kingdom, especially if we are willing and have a *yes* in our spirits, which Daniel and Eunice did. So God led them to Kampala, Uganda to help with an exciting new Kingdom project. Wow, South Koreans embracing the Kingdom in Africa! How wild is that?

As they shared the intriguing details of their story, they casually mentioned that that very day just happened to be the ten year anniversary of their arrival in Uganda.

It was then that they both admitted that, though they left South Korea because they were growing complacent, ten years later, they were finding themselves, once again, at the same place of complacency. Once more, they were choosing to ask God: what's next?

Complacency is horribly subtle, yet it has the power to render us passive. For me, the telltale sign of complacency is the lack of desire to spend time with other people. It is then I have a clear choice: to continue on the *it's all about me* journey, or to ask God a simple question: Who today? Or what's next?

Cynicism

My personal definition of *cynicism* is *being snarky—sarcastic, judgmental, cutting—rude to the face of, or behind the back of potentially anyone in my sphere.* This could include relatives, neighbors, co-workers, acquaintances, and the poor cashier at the grocery store, bless her.

The cynical responses first appear quietly in the mind, but, unchecked, it doesn't take long for the snark to float smoothly off the tongue. After that, it is virtually impossible to retrieve the gunk from the innocent's ears.

The true giveaway that cynicism has a hold in my life is when I begin talking back to the television, including the news, the commercials, and even the actors. Then it seeps over into my family as I give my unrequested opinion on today's latest newsflash. I feel clever and insightful, and that desire to make the listener hear me becomes insatiable.

Once I had an odd dream where several people from my past were suddenly in my house. A few of the guests were, in real life, literally deceased, so to see them, in my dream state, was shocking. However, I greeted each one of them with a smile and a hug. Near the end of the dream, I saw Rachael, who is very much alive. I approached her (with the realization that she was one of the few present who was, for sure, living) and whispered in her ear, "Why are you here?"

Quite casually she replied, "I am here to tell you that you don't realize how important and life-changing the consequences are from the little things that you are allowing in your life."

Then I woke up. I immediately knew exactly what Rachael was talking about. The subtle sarcasm and cynicism had crept into my everyday reactions. I easily rolled my eyes behind peoples' backs, made snide comments under my breath, and harshly judged the slightest infraction of strangers who were out of earshot. In other words, everything I was writing and even proclaiming was demeaned by the cynical remarks that I had so unwittingly allowed.

It had happened quickly, in the span of a gnat's breath. God used the dream to goad me back into His life, the Kingdom life, where I was created to live.

What We Do

We don't bring the Kingdom anywhere. Jesus already did that, so it is already here, all around us. The Kingdom lives in those who believe. We can't enlarge the Kingdom, nor add to it. However, we we are the ones that *bring the Kingdom news*.

When Jesus physically walked the planet over two thousand years ago, He spent a lot of time telling stories. One of these stories is about a farmer planting seed.

Most people, when asked, believe that the seed Jesus mentions represents salvation. However, salvation as we now understand it wasn't yet in existence.

Rather, Jesus said that the seed was "the news of the Kingdom."

He describes the four places that these seed could land:

- on the side of the road,
- in gravel (or rocky places),
- in weeds (or thorns), or
- in good soil.

Then Jesus ties this into how people respond to this *Kingdom news*:

> *When anyone hears news of the Kingdom and doesn't take it in, it just remains on the surface, and so the **Evil One comes along and plucks it right out of that person's heart.** This is the seed the farmer scatters on the road. The seed cast in the gravel—this is the person who hears and instantly responds with enthusiasm. But there is no soil of character, and so **when the emotions wear off and some difficulty arrives,** there is nothing to show for it. The seed cast in the weeds is the person who hears the kingdom news, but weeds of **worry and illusions about getting more and wanting everything** under the sun strangle what was heard, and nothing comes of it. The seed cast on good earth is the person **who hears and takes in the news, and then produces a harvest beyond his wildest dreams.***
> Matthew 13:19-23 MSG (bold, mine)

Seeds are normally small, some much smaller than others. Within each seed, life resides.

I once tossed some cantaloupe seed off of my side porch. The soil it landed in was obviously good—as was the amount of water and sunshine that it received. The life-filled seed was set up perfectly, so it did what seeds do: it shed its hard covering and began to shake, rattle, and roll. It took root, and it grew and took on a life of its own, apart from the original cantaloupe.

It grew so much that it turned into a large vine consuming the wall next to my driveway. Within weeks, tiny little cantaloupes began to show up on the vine, and then each of them grew and matured. Before long, I was harvesting ripe cantaloupes every day, each with hundreds of seeds, each capable of producing a harvest beyond my wildest dreams.

Jack

A seed in the Kingdom can be planted purposefully or accidentally. When I was 25 years-old, I volunteered in the office of a new church in Fort Worth, Texas. I was sitting in the tiny front room stuffing envelopes with the church secretary and Tim Taylor, one of the co-pastors.

It was then that Tim's father, Jack Taylor, who just happened to be the other pastor of the church, burst into the front door with his Bible open. It quickly became apparent that he was in preacher mode and before the door could shut behind him, he was preaching to the three of us!

"Do you know why God made the whales?" he propounded, not at all anticipating a reply.

I felt my eyebrows raise. Jack was one of my heroes of the faith, and I was a mere four feet from him as he began his inadvertent seed planting.

I slowly shook my head. Of course, I didn't know why God made the whales—or anything else for that matter.

In his distinctive, joy-filled voice, he continued, "It says here in Psalm 104, *'There the ships go to and fro, and Leviathan, which you formed to frolic there.'*"

He continued, "All these scientists have studied whales for years trying to figure out why they leap in and out of the ocean like they do, and yet here, clear as a bell, God says why he made them: He made them to frolic—to have fun! God made them so He could watch them jump around!"

With that last statement, Jack closed his Bible, walked past us, and went into his office. That seed fell on good ground. It was at that moment that I learned the art of considering. I learned the beauty of the hidden, small things, especially in Scripture. I learned that God is not only creative but fun. I learned that an accomplished man, even at age 50, could be teachable—like a child.

I also learned that I wanted more. I wanted to value small beginnings, small things, small choices, and small acts. I couldn't articulate it then, but I can now. What I wanted was the Kingdom: the place that God and His ways thrive. What I truly desired was for His Kingdom to come, to be realized, in me.

It has and it does.

A seed is small, a cup of cool water is small, choosing the worst seat in the room is a small act, as is hanging out with the smelliest person at the party. The person stacking chairs after an awards banquet gets no trophy. That is, unless they are seeking first the Kingdom.

Our Father which art in heaven,
Hallowed be thy name.

Thy kingdom come,
Thy will be done in earth,
as it is in heaven.

Give us this day our daily bread.

And forgive us our debts,
as we forgive our debtors.

And lead us not into temptation,
but deliver us from evil:
For thine is the kingdom, and the power,
and the glory, for ever.

Matthew 6:9-13 KJV

Final Thoughts

I was telling Hamilton, my third son, a very cool God-story. This one, like the many that I have told and have heard, had a very clear beginning and middle which were followed by an *Ah-Ha* ending.

He was working half-heartedly not to show it, but he was growing increasingly disinterested in my tale. *"Maybe he has other things to do,"* I thought. I took the cues and hurried the story along.

Whew, I was done.

As he kept his head down and his hands busy, I attempted to read his expression—*maybe perplexed, mixed with a touch of disdain?*

"What?" I blurted out. "What's wrong? I thought it was a very cool story."

"It was a cool story, Mom. It's just ...," he hesitated, as he was obviously wanting to choose his words carefully. "It's just that, with your generation, that's all that it is: *a cool story*. Because of that, you miss the fact that the story never ends. It continues. The story always continues, and you don't see that."

Ouch. He was correct.

Seeking the Kingdom never ends. All of the stories, mine and yours, are connected. So, seek the Kingdom. Tell the stories, but with a comma, not a period.

If you have made it to this final chapter, I want to bless you with a purposeful and provocative journey in seeking the Kingdom. The best and the most efficient way to obtain this blessing is to start small, today. You won't lose out on a thing.

Addendum: Kingdom Scriptures

Here are a few of my favorite Kingdom verses:

Once again the devil took him to a very high mountain, and from there showed him all the kingdoms of the world and their magnificence. "Everything there I will give you," he said to him, "if you will fall down and worship me."
Matthew 4:8-9 JBP

"Yes, and I tell you that tax-collectors and prostitutes are going into the kingdom of God in front of you!" retorted Jesus. "For John came to you as a saint, and you did not believe him—yet the tax-collectors and the prostitutes did! And, even after seeing that, you would not change your minds and believe him."
Matthew 21:31-32 JBP

Because of the spread of wickedness the love of most men will grow cold, though the man who holds out to the end will be saved. This good news of the kingdom will be proclaimed to men all over the world as a witness to all the nations, and the end will come.
Matthew 24:11-14 JBP

*The time has come at last—the kingdom of God has
arrived. You must change your hearts and minds
and believe the good news.*
Mark 1:14-15 JBP

*At daybreak, he went off to a deserted place,
but the crowds tried to find him and when they did
discover him, tried to prevent him from leaving them.
But he told them, "I must tell the good news of the
kingdom of God to other towns as well—that is my mission."
And he continued proclaiming his message
in the synagogues of Judea.*
Luke 4:42-44 JBP

*Don't be afraid, you tiny flock! Your Father plans
to give you the kingdom. Sell your possessions
and give the money away. Get yourselves purses
that never grow old, inexhaustible treasure in Heaven,
where no thief can ever reach it, or moth ruin it.
For wherever your treasure is, you may be certain
that your heart will be there too!*
Luke 12:32-34 JBP

*Later, he was asked by the Pharisees when the kingdom
of God was coming, and he gave them this reply:
"The kingdom of God never comes by watching for it.
Men cannot say, 'Look, here it is', or 'there it is,'
for the kingdom of God is inside you."*
Luke 17:20-21 JBP

You must let little children come to me, and you must never prevent their coming. The kingdom of God belongs to little children like these. I tell you, the man who will not accept the kingdom of God like a little child will never get into it at all.
Luke 18:16-17 JBP

"Believe me," returned Jesus, "a man cannot even see the kingdom of God without being born again."
John 3:3 JBP

My kingdom is not founded in this world—if it were, my servants would have fought to prevent my being handed over to the Jews. But in fact my kingdom is not founded on all this!
John 18:36 JBP

For after his suffering he showed himself alive to them in many convincing ways, and appeared to them repeatedly over a period of forty days talking with them about the affairs of the kingdom of God.
Acts 1:3 JBP

Then Paul made his way into the synagogue there and for three months he spoke with the utmost confidence, using both argument and persuasion as he talked of the kingdom of God.
Acts 19:8 JBP

*After all, the kingdom of Heaven is not a matter of
whether you get what you like to eat and drink, but
of righteousness and peace and joy in the Holy Spirit.*
Romans 14:17-18 JBP

*For I assure you, my brothers,
it is utterly impossible for flesh
and blood to possess the kingdom of God.
The transitory could never possess the everlasting.*
1 Corinthians 15:50 JBP

*For we must never forget that he rescued us
from the power of darkness, and re-established us in
the kingdom of his beloved Son,
that is, in the kingdom of light.
For it is by his Son alone that we have been
redeemed and have had our sins forgiven.*
Colossians 1:13-14 JBP

*The seventh angel blew his trumpet.
There arose loud voices in Heaven and they were
saying, "The kingship of the world now belongs
to our Lord and to his Christ, and he shall be king
for timeless ages!"*
Revelation 11:15 JBP

Suggested Reading

Cosmic Initiative: Restoring the Kingdom, Igniting the Awakening by Jack R. Taylor

Kingdom Journeys by Seth Barnes

A Tale of Three Kings by Gene Edwards

The Unshakeable Kingdom and the Unchanging Person by E. Stanley Jones

Unchanging and Unshakeable by Albert E. Jansen

About the Author

Karen Sillivant Dilbeck was born and reared in Charleston, South Carolina. She graduated from Winthrop College with a Bachelor of Arts in Art and Communications. Following an encounter with God's grace and mercy, she began working with teenagers at  her church and eventually moved to Ft. Worth, Texas to attend Southwestern Seminary. While there she met her husband, Tim. They married in 1984, and in 1985 Karen graduated with a Master of Arts in Communications.

Since teenagers were her first love, she continued working with them until 2008 in the two churches that her husband pastored for over 28 years. She also taught women's Bible Studies, spoke at various women's and youth functions, and led a weekly Bible study for teenage girls at a group home in downtown Montgomery, Alabama.

When she's not traveling, teaching, facilitating, counseling, or cooking, Karen enjoys gardening, reading, drawing, and writing. Karen's ultimate passion, though, remains seeking the Kingdom daily, especially in the most menial of things.

Karen and Tim have three grown sons, two daughters-in-law, a new grandbaby and a well-loved Brittany Spaniel named Rowe. Karen and Tim travel the world with Adventures in Missions where they help train and coach participants in the World Race. When not globetrotting, they entertain family and friends in their home in Cumming, Georgia.

Karen can be contacted at

StartSmallKingdom@gmail.com.

The God of heaven will set up a kingdom
that shall never be destroyed,
nor shall the kingdom be left to another people.
It shall break in pieces all these kingdoms and
bring them to an end, and it shall stand forever.
Daniel 2:44 ESV